EARTH
SCIENCE
DAYBOOK

In Collaboration with **NSTA**

GReat S**o**uRCe®
EDUCATION GROUP
A Houghton Mifflin Company

Acknowledgments

Reviewers

Michelle Stevens Krug
Coral Springs High School
Coral Springs, Florida

Richard Sturgeon
Glastonbury High School
Glastonbury, Connecticut

Maxine Rosenberg
Newton Public Schools
Newton, Massachusetts

Thomas Vaughn
Arlington Public Schools
Arlington, Massachusetts

Credits

Writing: Bill Smith Studio
Editorial: Great Source: Fran Needham, Marianne Knowles, Susan Rogalski; Bill Smith Studio
Design: Great Source: Richard Spencer; Bill Smith Studio
Production Management: Great Source: Evelyn Curley; Bill Smith Studio
Cover Design: Bill Smith Studio

National Science Teachers Association: Tyson Brown, Carol Duval, Juliana Texley, Patricia Warren

Photos

Page 4: PhotoDisc; **5:** PhotoDisc; **6:** PhotoDisc; **7:** PhotoDisc; **8:** PhotoDisc; **9:** ©Wampler Gaylon/CORBIS SYGMA; **11:** Painet; **12:** NASA; **13:** NASA; **14-15:** PhotoDisc; **16a:** NASA; **16b:** Corel; **17:** NASA; **18-19:** PhotoDisc; **20:** BSS; **20:** NASA; **22:** Corel; **22-23:** PhotoDisc; **24:** © Reuters New Media/CORBIS; **24:** © Reuters New Media/CORBIS; **25:** Corel; **26-27:** Corel; **28-29:** Corel; **30:** PhotoDisc; **32-33:** Corel; **34-35:** PhotoDisc; **36-37:** PhotoDisc; **38-39:** PhotoDisc; **40:** UCMP Berkley; **41:** ArtToday; **42-43:** PhotoDisc; **44:** PhotoDisc; **45:** PhotoSpin; **46-47:** PhotoDisc; **48:** © Layne Kennedy/CORBIS; **50:** Peter Sterling/taxi/Getty Images; **51:** Corel; **52:** Bettmann/CORBIS; **54-55:** PhotoSpin; **55:** PhotoSpin; **56:** Bettmann/CORBIS; **57:** PhotoSpin; **57:** Bettmann/Corbis; **58-59:** PhotoDisc; **60:** Bettmann/CORBIS; **61:** PhotoSpin; **62:** ArtToday; **63:** PhotoDisc; **64-65:** PhgotoDisc; **66-67:** Corel; **68-69:** PhotoDisc; **71:** USGS; **73:** © Bettman/CORBIS; **74-75:** BSS art; **77:** Princeton University/USGS; **81:** NOAA Central Library; **82:** PhotoDisc; **83:** Corel; **84-85:** PhotoDisc; **86:** ©Pedro Ugarte/ AFP/CORBIS; **87:** PhotoDisc; **88-89:** PhotoDisc; **90-91:** PhotoDisc; **92:** PhotoDisc; **93:** Corel; **94:** PhotoDisc; **97:** S. Mukerji, IDRC; **98-99:** PhotoDisc; **101:** PhotoDisc; **102-103:** PhotoDisc; **107:** PhotoDisc; **108-109:** Photodisc; **108a:** Friends of Quabbin; **108b:** Friends of Quabbin; **108c:** Les Campbell; **111:** PhotoDisc; **112-113:** PhotoDisc; **114:** Corel; **116-117:** PhotoDisc; **118:** ArtVille; **119:** Corel; **120-121:** PhotoDisc; **122:** Corel; **124:** PhotoDisc; **125:** W. James Ingraham, Jr/Beachcombers' Alert; **126-127:** PhotoSpin; **128:** PhotoSpin; **128:** PhotoSpin; **129:** PhotoDisc; **130-131:** Corel; **132-133:** PhotoDisc; **133:** PhotoDisc; **134:** © Tom Stewart/CORBIS; **135:** PhotoDisc; **136:** NOAA Central Library; **138:** PhotoSpin; **140-141:** PhotoDisc; **142:** NASA/GSFC/LaRC/JPL, MISR Team.; **144-145:** Corel; **146:** Corel; **148:** NASA; **148-149:** PhotoDisc; **150:** NOAA Central Library; **151:** Les Nagey; **151:** NOAA Central Library; **152-153:** PhotoDisc; **154:** Corel; **156-157:** PhotoDisc; **158-159:** PhotoDisc; **160:** © Layne Kennedy/CORBIS; **161:** PhotoDisc; **162-163:** PhotoDisc; **165:** Connecticut Historical Society; **166-167:** Corel; **168-169:** PhotoDisc; **170:** Corel; **171:** Corel; **171:** Corel; **172-173:** Corel; **174:** Corel; **175:** Corel; **176:** PhotoDisc; **177:** © Roger Ressmeyer/CORBIS; **178:** NASA; **179:** MIT Lincoln Laboratory; **180-181:** BSS; **182a:** University of Hawaii; **182b:** NASA; **184:** NASA; **186-187:** PhotoDisc; **188:** PhotoDisc; **189:** NASA; **190-191:** Corel; **192:** Corel; **192-193:** NASA; **194-195:** PhotoDisc; **196:** PhotoDisc; **199:** NASA; **200-201:** PhotoDisc; **202:** NASA; **205:** PhotoDisc; **206:** PhotoDisc; **208:** NASA/MSFC; **212:** PhotoDisc; **214:** NASA

Front cover: PhotoDisc   **Back cover:** Corel

Illustration: Thomas Gagliano, Technical Illustration; Page 10 map, Dan Stuckenschneider

Sources

12, 16 "Building a 3-D Map of Earth From Space!." *The Space Place.* California Institute of Technology/NASA. (spaceplace.jpl.nasa.gov/srtmmak2.htm)

20 "How Old Is Earth?." "Ask a Scientist" *MadSci Network.* Washington University Medical School. (www.madsci.org)

24 Bird, Dr. Peter. "Andy Gratz, a Scientist's Eulogy." Unpublished.

28 "pebbles" from ALL THE SMALL POEMS AND FOURTEEN MORE by Valerie Worth. Reprinted by permission of Farrar, Straus, & Giroux, LLC.

30 Hickam, Homer H., Jr. *Rocket Boys.* Delacorte Press Books for Younger Readers, a division of Random House, Inc.

34 "Energy Story: Geothermal Energy." *Energy Quest.* California Energy Commission. (www.energyquest.ca.gov/story/chapter11.html)

40, 44 "Mary Anning (1799-1847)." *University of California Museum of Paleontology.* The University of California Museum of Paleontology, Berkeley, and the Regents of the University of California. (www.ucmp.berkeley.edu/history/anning.html)

48 "Dinosaur Digs," Travel Channel, copyright Discovery Communications, Inc. All rights reserved. (www.discovery.com)

52 Cather, Willa. *O Pioneers!.* Houghton Mifflin.

52 From THE GRAPES OF WRATH by John Steinbeck, copyright 1939, renewed © 1967 by John Steinbeck. Used by permission of Viking Penguin, a division of Penguin Putnam Inc.

56 DUST STORM DISASTER Words and Music by Woody Guthrie. TRO—©Copyright 1960 [Renewed] 1963 [Renewed] Ludlow Music, Inc., New York, NY. Used by Permission.

62, 66 "Beach Erosion." The Why Files. Copyright 2002. University of Wisconsin Board of Regents.

70 U.S. Department of the Interior. "Dennis Dissipates, Work Just Begins for USGS Scientists." *United States Geological Survey.* (www.usgs.gov/public/press/public_affairs/press_releases/pr979m.html)

72 Hughes, Patrick. "The Meteorologist Who Started a Revolution." *Weatherwise.*

76, 80 *Naked Earth: The New Geophysics* by Shawna Vogel (Dutton, 1995; pp. 19-25). Reprinted by permission of Regula Noetzli Literary Agency.

82 U.S. Department of the Interior. "How Do Volcanoes Erupt?," *USGS Cascades Volcano Observatory.* (vulcan.wr.usgs.gov/Outreach/AboutVolcanoes/how_do_volcanoes_erupt.html)

86 Camp, Dr. Vic. "Mt. Pelée Eruption (1902)." *How Volcanoes Work.* Department of Geological Sciences, San Diego State University. (www.geology.sdsu.edu/how_volcanoes_work/Pelee.html)

88 Wood, Chuck. "Which Method Of Volcano Prediction Is The Most Useful And Reliable?." *Volcano World.* University of North Dakota. (volcano.und.nodak.edu/vwdocs/frequent_questions/grp3/question229.html)

96, 100 "In Person: Pilar Cereceda" by Maria de Luigi (www.idrc.ca). ©International Development Research Centre.

106 "The Quabbin Reservoir," *The Connecticut River Homepage.* University of Massachusetts Department of Biology. (www.bio.umass.edu/biology/conn.river/quabbinres.html)

110 Benson, Reed. "Stream of Consciousness." *WaterWatch.* (www.waterwatch.org/instream.html#STREAM)

114 Pachamama: Our Earth—Our Future (GEO-2000 for youth) UNEP. Year of publication: 1999. (www.unep.org/geo2000/pacha/fresh/fresh2.htm)

118 "Sweating the Small Stuff" (www.sciam.com/2001/0201issue/0201how/htm) ©Diane Martindale.

122 Fry, Sandra. "Icebergs to Africa." *Australian Broadcast Corporation.* (www.abc.net.au/news/features/antarctica/)

124 "Staying On Top: These Shoes Just Did It." *Ocean Planet.* Smithsonian Institution. (seawifs.gsfc.nasa.gov/OCEAN_PLANET/HTML/oceanography_currents_2.html)

128 Beach: Nike Shoes Wash Up by Janice Podsada, The Herald, 18 June 2001.

130 Gisvold, Magne. "'Water Mills' at the Bottom of the Sea." *SINTEF Publications.* SINTEF Energy Research. (www.sintef.no/publications/pro_eng_24.html)

138 Marion, Fulgence. *Wonderful Balloon Ascents: or the Conquest of the Skies.*

142 "Santa Ana Winds Swirl Over Southern California." NASA Jet Propulsion Laboratory. *California Institute of Technology.* (www.jpl.nasa.gov/releases/2002/release_2002_43.html)

146, 150, 154 From THE PERFECT STORM by Sebastian Junger. Copyright © 1997 by Sebastian Junger. Used by permission of W. W. Norton & Company, Inc.

156 Nelson, Allen. "Twisters: Destruction From the Sky." *ThinkQuest.* (tqjunior.thinkquest.org/4232/survivor.htm)

160 "HAIL, HAIL, HAIL—THE SUMMERTIME HAZARD OF EASTERN COLORADO" by Nolan J. Doesken, Assistant State Climatologist Colorado Climate Publication, April 1994, Volume 17, Number 7, Special Feature Association.

164 "Weatherlore." *Federal Writers' Project.* Library of Congress.

166 "Ancient tree rings reveal past climate." Reprinted with permission from SCIENCE NEWS, the weekly newsmagazine of science, copyright 2001 by Science Service Inc. (http://sciencenews.org/20010331/fob2.asp)

170 Armstrong, Sue. "Climate Change." *New Scientist.* (www.newscientist.com/hottopics/climate/climate.jsp?id=23154500)

172 "Thinning Sea Ice Stokes Debate on Climate Debate" by William K. Stevens (The New York Times, November 17, 1999). © 1999 The New York Times.

179 "An asteroid large enough to demolish. . ." Reprinted with permission of The Associated Press. (http://www.cbsnews.com/stories/2002/03/20/tech/main504213.shtml)

182 "Comet Meltdown!." *NASA Kids.* Center Operations Directorate at Marshall Space Flight Center. (kids.msfc.nasa.gov/news/2000/news%2Dlinear.asp)

184 "Stardust." *Liftoff. Science@NASA.* Marshall Space Flight Center. (liftoff.msfc.nasa.gov/academy/space/solarsystem/comets/stardust.html)

188 "Long Live Planet Pluto!." Reprinted with permission of The Associated Press.

192 "The Case of the Missing Mars Water." *Science@NASA.* Marshall Space Flight Center. (science.nasa.gov/headlines/y2001/ast05jan_1.htm)

198 "How Do We Determine The Life Cycles Of Stars And Tag Some As 'Young' And Some As 'Old'?." *Scientific American.*

202 Excerpted with permission from "Shadow of an Exoplanet Detected" by Govert Schilling, Science, 11-19-99. Copyright 1999 American Association for the Advancement of Science.

208 "Sailing to the Stars," *NASA Kids.* Center Operations Directorate at Marshall Space Flight Center. (kids.msfc.nasa.gov/news/2000/news%2Dsolarsail.asp)

212 Long, Michael. "Surviving in Space." *National Geographic.*

214 Letters to the Scientist. ©2002, The Scientist LLC. Reproduced with permission.

214 Letter to the Editor: "Concentrate on Earth." (www.the-scientist.com/yr2002/mar/let1_020304.html) © James R. Blevins, The Scientist, 16[5]: 13, Mar. 4, 2002.

214 Letter to the Editor: "On Earth and Travel to Mars, 1." (www.the-scientist.com/yr2002/apr/let_020401.html) © John F. Collins, The Scientist 16[7]: 14, Apr. 1, 2002.

UNIT 4 Weather and Climate

UNIT 1 Earth's Surface

Tiny things can lead to huge discoveries.

Who knew that you could learn about the extinction of dinosaurs by looking at microscopic crystals? Streaky layers in crystals are evidence of a major meteorite impact on Earth millions of years ago. Dust in the air may have blocked sunlight, killing plants. Plant-eating dinosaurs would have starved first, and then meat-eating dinosaurs.

In this unit you'll learn about Earth's surface and the stories it tells. Space-age technology is providing new ways to map the surface. By examining rocks, scientists can make inferences about the age and history of our planet. You'll explore some sources of energy that are hidden deep below the surface. And you'll find out how fossils—the remains and traces of ancient organisms—help tell Earth's stories.

? Did You Know?

Certain geologists, called "forensic geologists," use their knowledge of Earth's surface to help solve crimes. Mud or bits of rock stuck in a tire or on the bottom of someone's shoe can show that the person was at the scene of a crime. In some cases, suspects can be identified with no other clues.

What Earth Looks Like

Paradise Island!

How can you show the height of land features on a map?

A topographic map shows the elevations of surface features such as mountains and valleys. The elevation of a feature is its height above or below sea level. Topographic maps also include other natural features such as marshes, forests, and rivers. Structures such as roads, bridges, and buildings are also shown.

 **Explore**

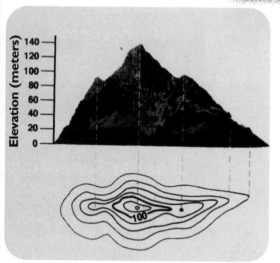

WHAT ARE CONTOUR LINES?

Topographic maps use contour lines to show the elevations of land features. A contour line connects points at the same elevation. All the lines have the same difference in elevation. That difference is called the *contour interval*.

Suppose you wanted to draw a topographic map of a mountain. First, you'd decide on a contour interval. Next you would measure to find points all around the mountain at the elevation of each contour interval. Then you'd draw a bird's-eye view of the mountain. Using your measurements, you'd draw one contour line to connect all the points at the elevation of one contour interval. Then you'd draw another contour line to connect all the points at the elevation of the next contour interval. You'd continue drawing contour lines like this until you had mapped the entire mountain.

▶ *What is the contour interval of the topographic map shown above?*

In some places on this map, the contour lines are closer together. In other places, the lines are farther apart.

▶ *What do you think a mountain looks like where the contour lines are closer together?*

▶ *What do you think a mountain looks like where the contour lines are farther apart?*

DRAW A MAP

What's your idea of the perfect island? Is it big or small? Does it have steep hills or flat beaches? Draw a topographic map of your island.

What You Need:

- drawing paper
- colored pencils

What to Do:

1. Sketch an outline of your island. Color the area around the island blue (for water).

2. Decide on a contour interval. If your island has steep hills, use a larger contour interval, such as 3 meters. If your island is not steep, use a smaller contour interval, such as 1 meter. Write the contour interval below your map.

3. Add contour lines to show elevations.

4. Add symbols to your map to show the location of each of the following:

map scale: ___cm = ___m	stream
[N↑] North arrow	■ house
woods (shade in green)	unpaved road
pond	sandy area

Think about where these features would belong in relation to the elevation of your land. (For example, streams would flow downhill, not sideways along ridges.)

5. Give your island a name.

What Do You Think?

► *If you were going for a hike, why would it be helpful to have a map with contour lines?*

_____

► *Trade maps with a classmate. Try to figure out what your classmate's island would look like. On a separate sheet of paper, describe your classmate's island.*

What Earth Looks Like

THE VIEW FROM THERE

Where can we get a bird's-eye view of our entire planet? From space!

The best way to make a map of an area is to have a bird's-eye view of it. Mapmakers and NASA space engineers have teamed up to make new topographic maps of Earth's surface.

People have drawn topographic maps for a long time. In 1879 U.S. Geologic Survey (USGS) mapmakers traveled on foot with pack mules to collect the data needed to draw maps. Today newer technologies are used to produce maps. Over the years, USGS has produced very detailed topographic maps of the entire United States. But even in the year 2000, such maps did not exist for most of the rest of the world. The solution? Use Space Shuttle data to map the rest of the world.

▲**Space Shuttle Endeavour**

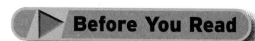

Before You Read

DRAW A MAP Use your memory to create a bird's-eye view of your neighborhood, school grounds, or another area you know well. Show the features and structures that would be seen from above. Use shading or patterns to show different kinds of surfaces, such as grass, trees, roofs, and roads.

▶ Read

NOTEZONE

<u>Underline</u> the words that describe the advantages of imaging radar over visible light telescopes.

Here's how the team collected the data they needed to show the surface details of nearly every place on Earth.

Making Maps From Space

The National Imagery and Mapping Agency of the U.S. Department of Defense, along with NASA,...are making the most detailed and accurate topographic map ever of almost the whole world. And they... gathered all the information for it in only 10 days!

The Shuttle Radar Topography Mission flew on the Space Shuttle Endeavour in February 2000. It used a technology called imaging radar. Imaging radar bounces a radar signal off the ground, then measures how long the signal takes to come back and how strong it is. From this information, we can make very accurate pictures of the surface, its bumps (like mountains, hills, and valleys), [and] its textures (like forests, lakes, and cities).... And imaging radar can see all this day or night, cloudy or clear.

Telescopes use [visible] light. Imaging radar uses a different kind of light, at a much longer, lazier wavelength that our eyes do not see. Radar can penetrate clouds. It passes right through them.

▲ **View of the Great Lakes from the Space Shuttle**

NASA: National Aeronautics and Space Administration, the U.S. agency in charge of spacecraft

texture: appearance of the surface—for example, smooth or bumpy

wavelength: the length of a wave from one high point to the next high point; different forms of light have different wavelengths

penetrate: go through

From: "Building a 3-D Map of Earth From Space!" *The Space Place.* California Institute of Technology/NASA. (spaceplace.jpl.nasa.gov/srtmmak2.htm)

FIND OUT MORE

SCIENCESAURUS

Showing Earth on Maps	166
Topographic Maps	172
Contour Lines	173
Topographic Map Symbols	174

SCILINKS.
THE WORLD'S A CLICK AWAY

www.scilinks.org
Keyword: Map Making
Code: GSED01

ANALYZING ADVANTAGES For many places on Earth, topographic maps are incorrect or do not exist. Some of these places are very hard to get to by land.

▶ **How does using the Space Shuttle to carry mapping equipment help solve this problem?**

_____

_____

▶ **What makes imaging radar a good way to collect mapping data from space?**

_____

INTERPRETING DIAGRAMS Like visible light hitting a mirror, radar signals move in straight lines. When they hit different Earth surfaces, the signals bounce—or reflect. If the surface is at a right angle to the signals, the signals will bounce back to the radar receiver. Signals that hit a surface at less than or greater than a right angle bounce away at the same angle and do not return to the radar receiver.

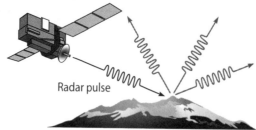

Radar pulse

This is the diagram that the team of mapmakers and space engineers uses to explain how they make topographic images from space.

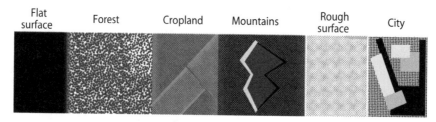

Flat surface   Forest   Cropland   Mountains   Rough surface   City

Each radar image shows the pattern that was formed by the radar signals. Dark areas show places that bounced back few signals. Bright areas show places that bounced back many signals.

▶ **Why would the image of a smooth road look dark?**

_____

_____

14

► Why would the image of a leafy forest look like a pattern of light and dark spots?

_____

_____

Look at the radar image of the mountains. One edge of the image is very bright.

► **What does this tell you about the surface at that part of the mountain?**

_____

_____

▷ Propose Explanations

GENERATING IDEAS With practice, scientists can interpret radar images and tell one kind of land surface from another. For example, imaging radar can show the difference between old lava flows and fresh lava.

► **How would this information be useful in describing a volcano?**

_____

_____

Imagine you are a scientist studying Earth's arctic regions. For several months of the year, these areas receive very little sunlight. The radar images show where ice on the ocean is thin and where it is thick.

► **How could these images be useful to ship owners?**

_____

_____

Imaging radar maps can show the boundaries of glaciers. The maps can also detect the thickness of the ice.

► **How might this information be useful to scientists studying changes in Earth's climate?**

_____

_____

_____

What Earth Looks Like

Viewing Earth With Two "Eyes"

What does it take to make a map showing the ups and downs of Earth's surface?

Using radar from space allows scientists to "see" and map Earth's surface through clouds and in the dark of night. But it is not so easy to see the elevations of the land on radar images. What scientists needed was a 3-D (three-dimensional) view of surface features such as volcanoes, valleys, and canyons. A 3-D view shows height as well as length and width. To get a 3-D image, you need two different views of the same thing. Your two eyes produce the 3-D images you see. NASA engineers had to come up with a way of collecting and using data from two different viewpoints in order to make a 3-D image.

▲ **Interferometry image of Mt. Cotopaxi, an active volcano in Ecuador**

Before You Read

TEST YOUR 3-D VISION Hold this book at arm's length. With both eyes open, center your nose over the small photo of Mt. Cotopaxi. Next, close one eye. Hold one arm out straight in front of you. Hold the thumb up so it completely hides the volcano. Now close that eye and open the other one. What do you notice? Why do you think that happens?

▼ **Mt. Cotopaxi**

_____

_____

_____

Read

NOTEZONE

Underline the words that tell how a 3-D image is made.

The NASA team solved the problem of how to get 3-D images of Earth's surface. Here's how they explain it.

Making Better Maps

We have flown imaging radar missions before and made radar images of different parts of the world.... But what was really new and special about the Shuttle Radar Topography Mission is that it combined imaging radar with another wonderful technology called interferometry....

The Shuttle Radar Topography Mission used interferometry by flying two separate radar antennas placed 60 meters apart! The mast that [held] the two radar antennas apart [was] the largest "unfolding" structure to ever fly in space.... When the mast [was] folded up inside the Space Shuttle bay for launch, it [was] only 3 meters long. That's like squashing basketball star Shaquille O'Neal from his normal 7-feet 1-inch down to only about 4 inches tall!

The "images" received by the two antennas [are] very carefully combined to give precise information about the height of the terrain below—in other words, to give a 3-D image! We end up with the best topographical map of the world ever made.

▲ Space Shuttle Endeavour maps topography of Earth

interferometry: using the interaction of waves to measure distances

antenna: a metal device used to send or receive signals

mast: a long pole that holds an object

precise: exact

terrain: ground

From: "Building a 3-D Map of Earth From Space!" *The Space Place.* California Institute of Technology/NASA. (spaceplace.jpl.nasa.gov/srtmmak2.htm)

FIND OUT MORE

SCIENCE**SAURUS**

Showing Earth
 on Maps   166
Topographic Maps 172
Contour Lines   173
Topographic Map
 Symbols   174

UNDERSTANDING SPACE AND TIME Here's a diagram that the NASA team uses to show how radar signals are transmitted and received aboard the Space Shuttle.

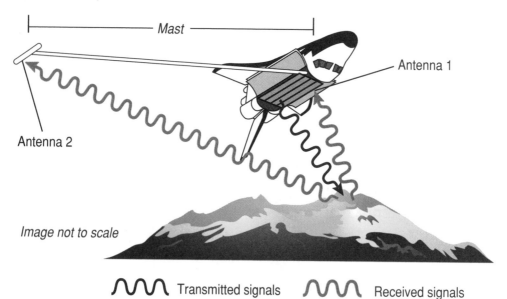

Transmitted signals   Received signals

▶ *From what are radar signals transmitted toward Earth's surface?*

_____

▶ *In what two places are the reflected radar signals received?*

_____

_____

MAKE INFERENCES

▶ *Based on what you see in the diagram, does the signal arrive at each antenna at the same time? If not, which antenna receives the signal first?*

_____

_____

▶ *How will the data from the two antennas be used to determine land height? (Hint: Think about what happened when you looked at the volcano picture with one eye at a time.)*

_____

_____

UNDERSTANDING THE SCIENCE-TECHNOLOGY CONNECTION Sometimes the challenges scientists face can result in the invention of a new technology. At other times a new technology will give scientists ideas for new investigations.

▶ *What challenge did the mapmakers have?*

_____

_____

▶ *How did NASA engineers use technology to meet that need?*

_____

_____

GENERATE IDEAS

▶ *Briefly explain how people in the following situations might use 3-D images from space.*

3-D Image Users	How They Could Use the Images
Pilots of small planes	
Backpackers	
Hang gliders	
Rescue workers	
Flood control engineers	
Scientists studying volcanoes	

Rock On!

Rock Clocks

How old is Earth? Ask a geologist!

Where do you go if you're a middle school student who wants to know the age of Earth? One idea is to go to an "ask-a-scientist" Web site. The question about Earth's age was sent to a geologist who studies rocks and the origin, history, and structure of Earth.

▶ Read

Here's the answer the geologist posted on the Web.

Question: How Old Is Earth?

Answer: According to geologists, Earth is about 4.5 billion years old. But the oldest rocks ever found on Earth are "only" about 3.8 billion years old. How did scientists arrive at 4.5 billion years as Earth's age? The process of plate tectonics "recycles" Earth's crust, so rocks as old as 4.5 billion years no longer exist. Since Earth formed at the same time as the rest of the solar system, scientists look at rocks that aren't from Earth. They study rocks taken from the moon by the Apollo missions, meteorites that fell to Earth, and very old igneous rocks present in Earth's crust.

Unlike Earth, the moon doesn't have plate tectonics. Rocks on its surface formed when the moon formed or arrived as meteorites from outer space. The oldest moon rocks and meteorites have been dated at about 4.5 billion years old.

Moon rock ▲

Scientists date the rocks by radiometric dating. They know that certain radioactive isotopes in rocks decay at a constant rate over time. They measure the amount of an

UNIT 1: EARTH'S SURFACE

isotope in a rock to get the rock's age. Igneous rocks form when molten magma solidifies. As the magma solidifies, certain radioactive isotopes become trapped. Scientists know the decay rate of the isotopes, so they can measure how much is left in the rock and determine its age.

Geologists and other scientists are still searching for rocks that may be older and could perhaps tell us more about the early solar system.

plate tectonics: the theory that Earth's crust is made of large sections that move on top of a softer, fluid layer

crust: outermost, rocky, solid layer of Earth

meteorite: a piece of rock that has fallen to Earth from space

igneous: rock formed from hot melted material that cooled

radioactive: giving off particles from its nucleus

isotope: an atom of a certain element with the same number of protons as other atoms of that element but a different number of neutrons

From: *MadSci Network.* Washington University Medical School. (www.madsci.org)

Explore

IDENTIFY SEQUENCES Geologists find most of the isotopes needed to do radiometric dating in igneous rocks. So they test igneous rocks from around the world, looking for the oldest rocks. To find out how igneous rocks form, look at this diagram of the rock cycle.

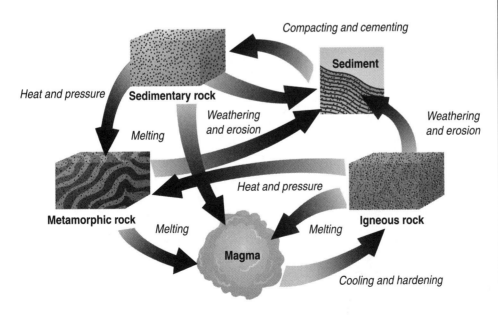

© GREAT SOURCE. COPYING IS PROHIBITED.

Examine the diagram on the previous page.

► *In what way can igneous rock form?*

_____

_____

_____

A rock's radioactive clock is reset each time rock changes to magma. Examine the diagram again.

► *Find six different sequences that result in the formation of magma. A sequence may have more than one change before it melts into magma. Fill in the table to organize your ideas. One example is shown.*

	ROCK TYPE AT START	HOW THE ROCK CHANGES	ROCK TYPE AFTER CHANGE	HOW THE ROCK CHANGES	CLOCK IS RESET
1	Sedimentary	melts			magma
2	Sedimentary				magma
3	Metamorphic				magma
4	Metamorphic				magma
5	Igneous				magma
6	Igneous				magma
7	Igneous				magma

▼ **Granite mountains**

Propose Explanations

SUPPORTING EVIDENCE Geologists often use evidence from one place to support conclusions about rocks they observe in other places. For example, observing layers in beach sand gives evidence to support how layers may have formed in a piece of sandstone found in a river canyon.

▶ *The actions of plate tectonics make rocks on Earth younger than Earth itself. According to the reading, what evidence do geologists use to support their conclusion? Where does that evidence come from?*

_____

_____

_____

_____

_____

_____

_____

_____

Take Action

WRITE DRAMATICALLY On a separate piece of paper, create a story that describes one of the rock sequences you identified in the chart. Use vivid language to describe how the rock was changed at each stage and the forces that changed it. When you are finished, write a sentence below explaining how your choice of words would be different if you were writing a scientific description rather than a dramatic one.

_____

_____

_____

_____

_____

_____

Rock On!

Crystal Conclusions

▲ Geologists inside a huge underground crystal cluster

What clues to Earth's history are in the crystals that make up rocks?

For many years, scientists have debated how the dinosaurs were wiped out 65 million years ago. At one time, the theory was that volcanic activity caused climate changes that killed the dinosaurs. In the past 25 years, scientists have gathered new evidence. This evidence supports the theory that dinosaurs died when a comet or meteor struck Earth, throwing dust particles into the air and blocking sunlight. Without sunlight, plants could not grow. Plant-eating dinosaurs starved, and then so did meat-eating dinosaurs. It takes the work of many scientists to investigate a new theory. Some of the evidence they find is as large as a crater. Some is as small as a microscopic crystal hidden inside a rock.

▷ Before You Read

SEEING PATTERNS Minerals are natural materials that make up Earth's rocks. Minerals have a crystal structure. Crystals are solids that show regular, repeating patterns of the same shape. Draw or describe other objects in nature that show regular, repeating patterns.

▶ **Read**

NOTEZONE

Underline the words that refer to the laboratory equipment that Andy used in his crystal research.

Andy Gratz was a geologist who studied crystals. He wondered whether any crystals might hold evidence about the impact theory of dinosaur extinction. Here's what Andy's college geology professor had to say about Andy.

Locked Up in Crystals

Andy's scientific passion was the secret life of crystals.... He took an interest in the [tiny] chips of quartz that are found around the world, in that centimeter-thick layer of clay that divides the Mesozoic world of dinosaurs from the Tertiary world of mammals. Specifically, he studied the strange textures called *lamellae* (which is Latin for "weird little streaky things") found only in these chips. At extreme magnification...he proved that these are tiny layers of glass, which...formed when the crystals were violently pulled apart by shocks. Then he [used] big machines to [shock some rocks and make more lamellae in the laboratory]. In this way, he put to rest the proposal that the crystals, and the catastrophe, were volcanic. From the intensity of the shock, he showed that they could result from nothing less than a major meteorite impact.... This result has been discussed around the world....This is truly fine detective work.

▼ **Copper sulfate crystal**

....

quartz: a hard, glassy mineral
Mesozoic: the time period in Earth's history from 230 million to 65 million years ago
Tertiary: the time period in Earth's history from 65 million to 2 million years ago

shock: in this case, a sudden shaking from something being hit very hard (not an electrical shock)
catastrophe: a terrible event

From: Bird, Dr. Peter. "Andy Gratz, a Scientist's Eulogy." Unpublished.

FIND OUT MORE

SCIENCESAURUS

Extinction	128
Minerals	179

THINK ABOUT IT

▶ *When Andy examined the crystals, what evidence did he find that they had been violently pulled apart by shocks?*

_____

_____

▶ *What did Andy do to model how the crystals formed?*

_____

_____

▶ *How did his results support the theory that it was a meteorite impact that caused the extinction of dinosaurs?*

_____

_____

_____

_____

NOTEZONE

Andy's professor used a metaphor to describe how Andy thought about what he read. Underline the words that describe the metaphor.

His professor had more to say about Andy's attitude as a research scientist.

Doubting Andy

[Andy] was skeptical, in the best way. When he would read what others had done, he would remember their experimental data, and file that in one part of his mind. In quite another place, he would file their conclusions, more as interesting gossip about the authors than as facts. He always maintained the firmest division between what we really know, and what we only like to pretend we know.

skeptical: doubting or questioning

From: Bird, Dr. Peter. "Andy Gratz, a Scientist's Eulogy." Unpublished.

PRACTICING SKEPTICISM Being skeptical is an important part of thinking like a scientist. A simple example from everyday life can help you understand why. Suppose you and your sister come home from school and find the kitchen table on its side. (Think of this as your data.)

▶ *Think of two different reasons (or conclusions) why the table got that way.*

_____

_____

_____

_____

▶ *Why do you think Andy was skeptical of the conclusions drawn by scientists?*

_____

_____

▷ Take Action

GENERATE QUESTIONS Andy Gratz was curious about crystals. All successful scientists have a great interest in the topics they investigate. Imagine that you will become a geologist.

▶ *Make a list of questions about Earth's surface, and processes that form it, that might interest you. Then describe how you think you might find the answers to those questions.*

_____

_____

_____

_____

_____

_____

_____

_____

Rock On!

PEBBLE POETRY

Every pebble tells a story.

The physical characteristics of a pebble tell us something about how it was formed and what happened to it in its long journey to your hand. "Reading" a pebble lets you get to know its history.

 **Read**

Here is a poem about pebbles that might have a story to tell you.

Pebbles

Pebbles belong to no one
Until you pick them up—
Then they are yours.

But which, of all the world's
Mountains of little broken stones,
Will you choose to keep?

The smooth black, the white,
The rough gray with sparks
Shining in its cracks?

Somewhere the best pebble must
Lie hidden, meant for you
If you can find it.

From: Worth, Valerie. "Pebbles." *All the Small Poems and Fourteen More.* Farrar, Straus, & Giroux.

FIND OUT MORE

SCI
LINKS
THE WORLD'S A CLICK AWAY

www.scilinks.org
Keyword: Identifying Rocks and Minerals
Code: GSED03

Activity

GET TO KNOW A PEBBLE

Look closely at a pebble. What can you infer about its history?

What You Need:
- pebble
- magnifier
- water

What To Do:

1. Find a pebble that you would like to "make your own."

2. Use the magnifier to look closely at your pebble. Rub a little water on the surface to bring out any patterns that might be there.

3. In the chart, record the physical characteristics of your pebble—its shape, color, surface texture (rough or smooth), hardness, layers or bands, whether it contains crystals or has marks on the surface, and any other things you notice.

4. Think about the characteristics that might tell you about the pebble's history. For example, how did its "mother" rock form? How long ago was your pebble separated from the "mother" rock? How has it changed? Where has it traveled? Has it been in water? Write your inferences in the chart.

What Do You See?

Pebble Characteristic	Inferences About the Pebble's History

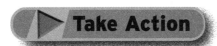
Take Action

WRITE YOUR PEBBLE'S STORY On a separate sheet of paper, write a poem that describes your pebble's history from its beginning as part of the "mother" rock to your hand. Include the characteristics you observed. Don't forget to give your poem a title.

Energy Resources

DIGGING UP ENERGY

What lies hidden in the dark, deep below Earth's surface? A source of light!

Much of our electricity comes from burning fossil fuels—coal, oil, and natural gas. Fossil fuels form over millions of years from the remains of dead organisms. Because they take such a long time to form, these fuels are called *nonrenewable resources*.

▶ **Read**

NOTEZONE

In the box, sketch a diagram showing the coal seam, draw rock, and jack rock.

In the mid-1800s, American coal miners began to work in deep underground mines. Homer Hickam grew up during the 1950s in a West Virginia coal mining town. He made his first trip into a coal mine at the age of 15. Homer described his trip like this.

Into the Coal Mine

I was almost shaking with excitement. I'd lived in Coalwood my whole life, but had never been where Dad was going to take me. I was going into the mine!

"Come over here," he beckoned, spreading a map of the mine on the table. He pointed at a winding black streak that ran across it. "That's the Number Four Pocahontas Seam, the finest and purest soft coal in the world. These lines I've drawn represent the tunnels we've driven through it since the mine has been operational."

He...brought out another drawing. "This is the side view of a typical seam. The coal is overlaid by a hard shale called draw rock. Underneath is what we call jack rock. Engineers have to know how to hold up the draw rock to keep it from falling and how to move the jack rock out of the way...."

The attendant swung the gate aside, and for the first time in my life I stepped onto the wooden-plank platform of the lift.... The boards in the floor were set apart enough that I could see between them. There was nothing beneath us but a dark chasm.... The man-hoist winch began to creak and the lift dropped quickly, my stomach lifting up around my throat. I grabbed Dad's arm, then quickly let go in embarrassment.... I watched the solid rock of the shaft slip by.... We were being swallowed by the earth, and I hadn't decided yet whether I liked that.

FIND OUT MORE

SCIENCE SAURUS

Fossil Fuels   325

---

beckoned: signaled

operational: in use

shale: fine-grained rock formed from mud or clay

attendant: a helper in charge of something (in this case, a gate)

chasm: a deep opening in the ground

man-hoist: a device to lower and raise workers in a narrow space

winch: a crank used to move the hoist

shaft: a long, vertical passage

From: Hickam, Homer H., Jr. *Rocket Boys.* Delacorte Press Books for Younger Readers, a division of Random House, Inc.

▶ **Explore**

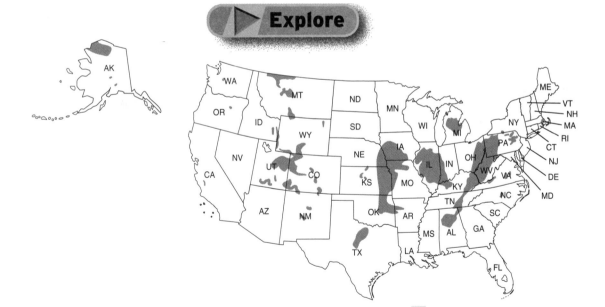

Coal deposits

FIND THE COAL The map shows where coal deposits are located in the United States.

▶ *Where are the largest coal deposits?*

_____

_____

▶ *How important do you think coal mining was to the economy of West Virginia (WV), where the Hickam family lived? Explain.*

_____

_____

_____

The coal mined by Homer's dad and other men in the 1950s was sold to steel-making companies in Pennsylvania, Ohio, and Indiana. The coal was needed as fuel for furnaces used in steel manufacturing.

▶ *How can you explain the choice to build steel plants in these three states?*

_____

_____

_____

One hundred years ago, coal was used mainly to heat homes and to power railroads and factories. Today, almost all the coal mined in the United States is burned to produce electricity. The table shows what percentage of electric power is generated from each fossil fuel in 14 states.

Percent of Electricity from Fossil Fuels			
State	% from Coal	% from Oil	% from Gas
Alabama	62	0	4
Alaska	10	8	68
California	1	1	51
Idaho	0	0	2
Illinois	47	0	3
Kentucky	97	0	0.5
Missouri	82	0	4
Montana	74	1	0
North Carolina	32	1	1
Oklahoma	64	0	32
Pennsylvania	59	2	2
Texas	36	1	52
Vermont	0	1	1
West Virginia	98.8	0.2	0.2

Adapted and edited from "State by State: Percentage of Total Electricity Generation" (2000) by the Nuclear Energy Institute

WHAT DO YOU THINK? Look at the table on the opposite page and the map on page 31 to answer the following questions.

► Notice that only 1 percent of California's electrical energy comes from coal. Why do you think this percentage is so small?

_____

_____

► Notice that 98.8 percent of West Virginia's electrical energy comes from coal. Why do you think this percentage is so large?

_____

_____

► Which state in the table depends most on fossil fuels for electric power? (Hint: Add up the percentages for all three fuels.)

_____

► Notice that none of the states depend entirely on fossil fuels to generate electricity. What are some other energy sources these states might use?

_____

_____

▶ Take Action

WRITE HOMER'S JOURNAL ENTRY Imagine what 15-year-old Homer Hickam, Jr., wrote in his journal the night after entering a coal mine with his father for the first time. How did he feel about being underground? Do you think he wants to go back underground for a visit or to work?

_____

_____

_____

_____

_____

Energy Resources

THE HEAT IS ON

Hot water is good for more than just taking baths!

Scientists are always looking for sources of energy that we can use without using them up. Energy sources that cannot be used up are called *renewable resources*. Hot springs and geysers like Yellowstone's Old Faithful are one clue that there is heat energy within Earth's crust. In some places, that energy can be used to produce electricity. One of those places is California.

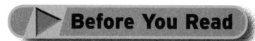
▶ Before You Read

HEAT ON THE MOVE Heat energy is energy related to the temperature of a substance. Heat energy is transferred between materials at different temperatures. Heat energy always moves from a warmer material to a cooler one. Within Earth, heat energy moves from warmer rock to cooler water, heating the water.

▶ *Describe three situations in your home or school in which heat energy is transferred from one material to another.*

_____

_____

_____

_____

_____

▲ **Old Faithful**

▶ Read

Here's what you can learn about geothermal energy on California's energy Web site.

Energy From the Earth

Below the crust of Earth, the top layer of the mantle is hot [soft] rock called magma.... Deep under the surface, water sometimes makes its way close to the hot rock and turns into hot water or into steam. The hot water can reach temperatures of more than...148 degrees Celsius. This is hotter than boiling water....

In some places, like in San Bernardino in southern California, hot water from below ground is used to heat buildings during the winter.... [Other areas, such as the Geysers area north of San Francisco,] have so much steam and hot water that it can be used to generate electricity. Holes are drilled into the ground and pipes lowered into the hot water, like a drinking straw in soda. The hot steam or water comes up through these pipes from below ground....

Like a [fossil fuel] power plant, where a fuel is burned to heat water into steam, the steam in a geothermal power plant goes into a special turbine. The turbine blades spin and the shaft from the turbine is connected to a generator to [produce] electricity.... The electricity then goes to huge transmission wires that link the power plants to our homes, schools, and businesses.

crust: Earth's surface layer
mantle: the layer of Earth below the crust
turbine: a machine that converts heat energy to mechanical energy
shaft: a rotating bar that connects two objects

generator: a machine that converts mechanical energy to electrical energy
transmission wires: wires that carry electrical energy from one place to another

From: "Energy Story: Geothermal Energy." *Energy Quest.* California Energy Commission. (www.energyquest.ca.gov/story/chapter11.html)

INTERPRETING A MAP Geothermal energy sources are found only in certain areas of the United States. The map below shows those areas.

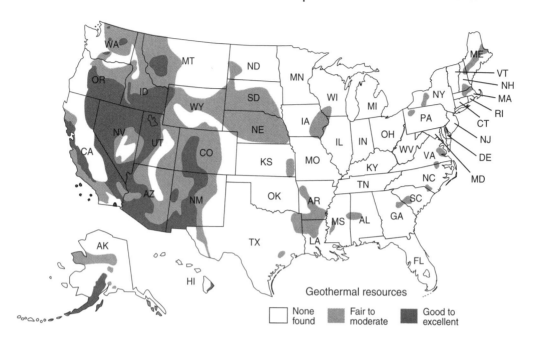

Geothermal resources

☐ None found ▨ Fair to moderate ■ Good to excellent

▶ *In what area of the U.S. are most geothermal energy sources located?*

_____

_____

▶ *Why do you think geothermal energy sources occur in some places but not in others?*

_____

_____

_____

_____

_____

_____

_____

_____

DEFINING RESOURCES Some of the heat inside Earth is left over from the formation of our planet over 4 billion years ago. Most heat inside Earth comes from the radioactive decay of elements in rocks. In some places, water moves through Earth's crust, deep enough to be heated. Geothermal power plants are built where the hot water is near enough to the surface to reach by drilling wells. Once the heat energy is removed, the water can be pumped back down into the ground where it is reheated. The heat energy used in this way is more than replaced by Earth's crust.

Renewable resources are those that can be replaced. Inexhaustible resources are those that people cannot use up, no matter how much they use.

▶ *In what way is geothermal energy an inexhaustible resource?*

_____

_____

▶ *In what way is geothermal energy a renewable resource?*

_____

_____

Take Action

THINK CREATIVELY Only underground water heated above 150°C is hot enough to be used for generating electrical energy. But water heated to between 20°C and 150°C can also be used as an energy source. Water in this temperature range can be piped to homes and greenhouses to heat them.

▶ *List your ideas for more ways to use geothermal energy. Keep in mind what both city dwellers and people who live in the country might need. Also think about things that might limit the distance that geothermal energy could be transported.*

_____

_____

_____

_____

_____

_____

_____

Energy Resources

Energy Choices

Is there a best way to produce electricity? You decide.

Electrical energy can be generated from either nonrenewable energy sources such as coal or from renewable energy sources such as geothermal energy. Each source has its benefits and its drawbacks. It's up to citizens to weigh the pros and cons of each source and make the best decision.

 **Explore**

ELECTRICITY NEEDS Most communities rely on a dependable supply of electricity. Make a concept map to show the uses of electricity in your home or in your school.

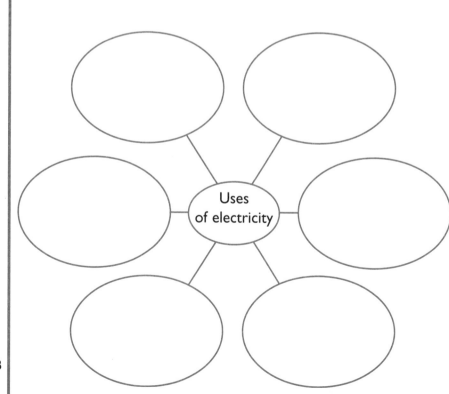

Uses
of electricity

Activity

CONSIDER YOUR OPTIONS This chart compares two ways of producing electricity—from coal and from geothermal energy.

	Electricity from Coal	Electricity from Geothermal Energy
Energy source	Burn coal to produce steam	Steam and hot water from heat in Earth's crust
Availability of fuel source	Coal is plentiful and cheap.	Mostly limited to parts of western states, Alaska, and Hawaii
Location of plant	Can be built just about anywhere that coal can be delivered by ship or railroad	Needs to be near a geothermal source that can be reached by drilling wells
Pollution	Large amounts of carbon dioxide and sulfur dioxide	Steam and tiny amounts of carbon dioxide and sulfur dioxide; poisonous heavy metals in water; noise pollution
Space	Large facility required	Small facility required
Cost to customer	$0.035–$0.04 per kilowatt-hour	$0.05–$0.08 per kilowatt-hour
Disruption to land	Most coal mining today requires stripping away land surface.	Wells drilled into ground for steam to rise up through
Transportation and storage of fuel	Need to ship in and store large amounts of coal	No transportation or storage needed
Power plant maintenance	High cost to obtain and transport coal	Low cost (Steam and hot water are free.) Maintenance can be high due to corrosiveness of water.
Reliability	Generating electrical energy 60–70% of the time	Generating 95% of the time
Long-term sustainability	There is a limited amount of coal on Earth.	Earth's heat is unlimited.

Imagine that you live in a western state where there are good geothermal energy sources. Your region needs a new power plant. One citizens' group proposes a coal-fired plant. Another group proposes a geothermal plant.

▶ *You've been asked to interview both groups for a report in the newspaper. Using the table for ideas, list questions that you would ask both groups. Your goal is to report on the plans for both types of plants without trying to influence the readers about which plant is a better choice.*

_____

_____

_____

Fossil Hunters

SHE SELLS SEASHELLS

Can a self-taught person do *real* science? Mary Anning did.

Back in the 1800s, few girls went to school—especially those who came from poor families. Despite the disadvantages she faced, young Mary Anning of Lyme Regis, England, learned to think scientifically. As a result, she made a valuable contribution to paleontology, the study of fossils. Fossils are the remains or traces of organisms that lived on Earth thousands or millions of years ago.

▲ **Mary Anning**

Before You Read

ORGANIZE YOUR IDEAS What kinds of things can become fossils? How does something become "fossilized"?

▶ *Record your ideas below. Draw a picture of a fossil you might have seen.*

UNIT 1: EARTH'S SURFACE

NOTEZONE

Underline the
words that
tell what
made Mary
Anning a
successful
fossil hunter.

Fossil collecting was the Anning family's business.

A Family Business

Mary Anning was born in 1799 to Richard and Mary Anning of Lyme
Regis...on the southern shores of Great Britain. The cliffs at Lyme Regis
were—and still are—rich in spectacular fossils from the seas of the
Jurassic period.... Richard was a cabinetmaker and occasional fossil
collector. Unfortunately, Richard died in 1810, leaving his family in debt
[and] without a provider. He did, however, pass on his fossil hunting
skills to his wife and children....

The Anning family lived in poverty and anonymity, selling fossils
from Lyme Regis.... By the middle of the 1820s, daughter Mary had
established herself as the keen eye and accomplished anatomist of the
family, and began taking charge of the family fossil business....

Mary Anning...help[ed] to discover
the first specimen of *Ichthyosaurus* to
be known by the scientific community
of London. This specimen was probably
discovered sometime between 1809 and
1811, when Mary was only 10 to 12 years
old.... Mary's skill and dedication

▼ **Ichthyosaurus
fossil**

produced many remarkable finds and thus provided the fatherless family
with a means of income. It is clear...that Anning was not only a collector,
but was well-versed in the scientific understanding of what she collected,
and won the respect of the scientists of her time. Her discoveries were
important in reconstructing the world's past and the history of its life.

---

spectacular: unusually good or
impressive

Jurassic: the time period from 208
million to 144 million years ago

anonymity: not being known or
recognized by others

anatomist: a person who studies
the structure of organisms

specimen: an individual that is
thought to be typical of its kind

Ichthyosaurus: an extinct ocean
reptile with a fishlike body and
paddlelike limbs

dedication: commitment

FIND OUT MORE

SCIENCE SAURUS

Rocks	180
Fossils	198

*SCi*LINKS.
THE WORLD'S A CLICK AWAY

www.scilinks.org
Keyword: Fossils
Code: GSED06

From: "Mary Anning (1799-1847)." *University of California Museum of Paleontology.* The University of
California Museum of Paleontology, Berkeley, and the Regents of the University of California.
(www.ucmp.berkeley.edu/history/anning.html)

MAKING INFERENCES In the 1820s, Mary Anning walked the beaches and climbed the cliffs of Lyme Regis. But 200 million years earlier, the rock of Lyme Regis was located at the bottom of the ocean.

The ocean then was full of many types of organisms. Today we know many of these ancient organisms only as fossils. *Ichthyosaurs*, like the fossilized one Mary Anning found, were plentiful. When the organisms died, their remains sank to the ocean floor. In that part of the ocean, the water was calm and shallow, and the remains stayed where they were. Some remains became trapped in sand and mud. Over millions of years, pressure, compacting, and cementing turned the sand and mud to stone. The organisms' remains were fossilized in the stone.

▶ *Why were there so many fossils in the cliffs of Lyme Regis?*

_____

_____

_____

_____

▶ *Think about conditions on the ocean shore. Why do you think there were more fossils to be found along the beaches at the base of the cliffs in Lyme Regis than in other places around town?*

_____

_____

_____

▶ *Scientific discoveries are often made when a person with the right knowledge is in the right place at the right time. In what ways was Mary Anning in the right place at the right time? In what ways was she the right person?*

_____

_____

_____

_____

_____

_____

THINKING LIKE A SCIENTIST

▶ *Based on what you read, what do you think was one reason Mary Anning started collecting fossils?*

_____

_____

▶ *In what ways was Mary Anning like a scientist today?*

_____

_____

▶ *In what ways was Mary Anning not like most scientists today?*

_____

_____

CONDUCT AN INTERVIEW Imagine that you are a reporter from a scientific magazine who will interview Mary Anning. What questions would you ask about her life and fossil hunting? List the questions below. What do you think her responses might be? On a separate sheet of paper, write your report of the interview.

_____

_____

_____

_____

_____

_____

_____

_____

_____

Fossil Hunters

Markers of Time

▲ Trilobite fossil

What makes a scientist's work extraordinary?

Scientists of Mary Anning's time were shocked when they heard of the work of the young fossil hunter. In the early 1800s, a person from a poor family did not think of being a scientist. And a female scientist? Next to impossible!

▶ Before You Read

THINK ABOUT IT Every fossil is like one piece of the puzzle of Earth's history.

▶ *What do fossil hunters need to do to make their fossils count as pieces of this puzzle?*

_____

_____

_____

_____

_____

_____

_____

_____

NoteZone

<u>Underline</u> all the descriptions of how Mary Anning acted like a scientist.

▶ **Read**

Here's what one of Mary Anning's fans—a wealthy woman—wrote in her diary in 1824 after seeing how Mary worked with fossils.

An Extraordinary Young Woman

The extraordinary thing in this young woman is that she has made herself so thoroughly acquainted with the science that the moment she finds any bones she knows to what tribe they belong. She fixes the bones on a frame with cement and then makes drawings and has them engraved.... It is certainly a wonderful instance of divine favour— that this poor, ignorant girl should be so blessed, for by reading and application she has arrived to that degree of knowledge as to be in the habit of writing and talking with professors and other clever men on the subject, and they all acknowledge that she understands more of the science than anyone else in this kingdom.

acquainted: familiar

tribe: in this case, a classification group

fixes: attaches

engraved: prepared for printing

divine favour: the idea that God acted to help someone

ignorant: not educated

application: hard work

kingdom: country ruled by a king or queen

From: "Mary Anning (1799-1847)." *University of California Museum of Paleontology*. The University of California Museum of Paleontology, Berkeley, and the Regents of the University of California. (www.ucmp.berkeley.edu/history/anning.html)

Ammonite fossils ▶

FIND OUT MORE

SCIENCESAURUS

Rocks	180
Geologic Principles	195
Fossils	198

SCiLINKS
THE WORLD'S A CLICK AWAY

www.scilinks.org
Keyword: Fossils
Code: GSED06

UNDERSTANDING THE WORK OF SCIENTISTS Mary Anning did not go to school to learn to be a scientist. Yet she acted like one in the field.

► *According to the reading, how did Mary Anning develop her skills as a scientist?*

_____

_____

► *How did Mary Anning record her findings?*

_____

► *How did Mary Anning display the fossils for scientists to study?*

_____

_____

► *How did Mary Anning make her discoveries available to scientists?*

_____

_____

Over the years, Mary Anning's knowledge grew as she saw more fossils.

► *How do you think seeing so many fossils helped her understand them?*

_____

_____

_____

WHAT DO YOU THINK? Some people collect natural objects just to have a collection or to sell. Other collectors do more. They keep detailed records of their finds, learn about their collections, and share what they learn. By doing so, they may add to scientific knowledge.

► *Which type of collector was Mary Anning? Why do you think so?*

_____

_____

_____

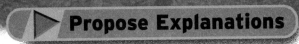

Propose Explanations

MAKING INFERENCES Earth's surface has constantly changed over billions of years. Continents that were once joined have been separated and then joined again. Rocks that were once under the ocean have been pushed up and today are dry land. New layers of rock have formed on top of older layers and then have been covered by even newer layers. Rocks on land have been pushed under the ocean. By studying fossils, scientists can make inferences about Earth's history.

▶ *Imagine that you are studying the fossil data described below. For each piece of evidence, write an inference you can make about Earth's history or the age of a rock layer.*

Evidence	Inference
Fossils of the same kind of land animals are found on different continents.	
Fossils of organisms that lived on coral reefs are found on the plains of Iowa.	
Coral-reef fossils are found in rocks on a mountaintop in Canada.	
Fossil A is found in a lower layer of rock than Fossil B.	
Fossils of a kind of organism that lived for only a short time 400 million years ago are found at different locations around the world.	

Fossil Hunters

Against All Odds

Even a retired science teacher on vacation can make a contribution to science.

Mary Anning became a respected fossil hunter. Can someone living today do the same thing? Lou Tremblay did. He's a retired earth science teacher who volunteers to help scientists looking for fossils.

Read

On a field trip in Montana, Mr. Tremblay made quite a discovery.

Dinosaur Dig

Lou Tremblay, a dinosaur dig volunteer, noticed nothing but the ground two feet [60 cm] in front of him. "I was determined to make a find," he recalls…. So Tremblay, with head hung low and eyes fixed downward, paced over baked brown clay until finally he stopped, stooped, and scooped up what looked like a bone fragment….

But that was just the beginning. Using [soft] paintbrushes, he and [a] fellow volunteer…cleared away surface dirt to discover that this knob was the weathered tip of a long, slender bone. As they had been taught in field school, they snapped some photos, noted their location in a logbook, and loosened some surrounding soil with a scratch awl. "At this point we knew it was something big," Tremblay says….

Some weeks later…Keith Rigby, a paleontologist at the University of Notre Dame, told Tremblay that the rib he found, along with a pelvis, claw, and toe bone found nearby, clearly belonged to a large carnivorous dinosaur. Tremblay's find may even be the largest tyrannosaur specimen ever found.

scratch awl: a hand tool with a sharp point
paleontologist: a scientist who studies fossils to learn about organisms of the past

pelvis: the bones at the base of the spine where the legs are attached to the body
carnivorous: meat-eating

From: "Join a Dig." *Dinosaur Digs*. Travel Channel.
(travel.discovery.com/ideas/outdoors_parks/dinodigs/join.html)

Explore

MAKING INFERENCES Mr. Tremblay volunteers to work at fossil digs run by paleontologists. The scientists run a field school before allowing the volunteers to dig.

▶ *Why do you think the volunteers need to go to the field school before digging for fossils?*

_____

_____

_____

▶ *What do you think scientists teach the volunteers at the field school?*

_____

_____

_____

▶ *Volunteers are not allowed to take fossils home. Why do you think that is the case?*

_____

_____

_____

▶ *How did Mr. Tremblay, who was not a paleontologist, contribute to scientific knowledge?*

_____

_____

_____

Take Action

LEAVE THE BONES ALONE! Imagine that you are a park ranger in an area where fossilized bones are often found. On a separate sheet of paper, write a paragraph for the park brochure telling visitors what they should do if they find a fossil. Explain why they should not take the fossil.

Dynamic Earth

There's never a dull moment here on Earth!

Earth's surface is continuously changing. Things shift, wash away, scatter in the wind, and sometimes explode. Things we take for granted—even major things like the position of Earth's continents—haven't always been the way they are now. And they won't be the same hundreds, thousands, or millions of years from now, either!

In this unit you'll explore some ways that Earth's surface changes. You'll see how wind and water move soil and sand from one place to another. You'll learn about the evidence that scientists used to determine that Earth's continents move over time. And you'll find out what makes some volcanoes explode in a violent eruption.

? Did You Know?

In 1883, the most powerful volcanic eruption in
recorded history blew away most of the island of
Krakatoa in Indonesia. Waves 37 meters (120 feet)
high killed 36,000 Indonesians. People in Australia over
3,200 kilometers (2,000 miles) away reported hearing
the explosions. A huge dust cloud rose 80 kilometers
(50 miles) into the atmosphere, blocking sunlight
worldwide and lowering temperatures by one degree.

Conserving Soil

Blown Away

To most of us, soil is just the material that covers the ground. But to farmers, it's the source of their livelihood.

Farmers who settled much of the Great Plains in the late 1800s were amazed by the soil they found. It was deep, dark, rich, and almost free of rocks. Unlike the eastern United States, where farms were on hilly, rocky ground surrounded by forest, the level land had only a few trees to cut down.

After farmers had plowed through the thick tangle of wild grasses, they planted wheat and corn in the bare soil. After the harvest, the fields were left unplanted. The farmers thought that giving the soil a rest promised a good crop next year, too. They also believed this wonderful topsoil would be there forever. But they were wrong.

Before You Read

THINK ABOUT IT The rich soil of the Great Plains took thousands of years to form. As the wild grasses died, nutrients from the rotting plants became part of the soil. Each year young grasses sprouted up through the decaying stems and roots. Plowing did two things. It broke up the tangled plants and roots that held the surface soil together. It also cut deeply into the land, loosening packed soil and bringing it to the surface.

► *What can happen to soil after it is plowed? How might weather conditions such as rain, drought, and wind affect the plowed soil?*

_____

_____

_____

_____

UNIT 2: DYNAMIC EARTH

▶ Read

Farming the Great Plains

Willa Cather wrote about farming on the Great Plains of Nebraska in the early 1900s. Here's what she said.

There are few scenes more [pleasing] than a spring plowing...where the furrows of a single field often lie a mile in length, and the brown earth, with such a strong, clean smell, and such a power of growth and fertility in it, yields itself eagerly to the plow.... The wheat-cutting sometimes goes on all night as well as all day, and in good seasons there are [hardly enough] men and horses...to do the harvesting. The grain is so heavy that it bends toward the blade and cuts like velvet.

In the 1930s, disaster struck. It did not rain, and the soil dried in the hot sun. Winds picked up the dry soil and blew it into the air. Here's how writer John Steinbeck described the dust storms.

Now the wind grew strong and hard and it worked at the rain crust in the corn fields. Little by little, the sky was darkened by the mixing dust, and the wind felt over the earth, loosened the dust, and carried it away. The wind grew stronger. The rain crust broke and the dust lifted up out of the fields and drove gray plumes into the air like sluggish smoke. The corn threshed the wind and made a dry, rushing sound. The finest dust did not settle back to earth now, but disappeared into the darkening sky.

furrow: a shallow trench left by a plow
fertility: the ability to support much plant life
yields: gives in

rain crust: the thin top layer of soil that hardened after light rain
plume: resembling a feather
sluggish: slow, lazy
threshed: struck over and over again

top: From: Cather, Willa. *O Pioneers!* Houghton Mifflin.
bottom: From: Steinbeck, John. *The Grapes of Wrath.* Penguin Putnam.

NOTEZONE

This reading tells about planting and harvesting crops. Circle the sentences that describe planting. Underline the sentences that describe harvesting.

What happened to the finest dust?

FIND OUT MORE

SCIENCESAURUS

Weathering, Soil,
and Erosion   188
Soil   191
Erosion and
Deposition   192

www.scilinks.org
Keyword: Wind Erosion
Code: GSED07

COMPARE AND CONTRAST

▶ *Willa Cather and John Steinbeck describe the soil of the Great Plains very differently. Compare their descriptions. How did soil conditions change from 1900 to the 1930s?*

_____

_____

_____

INTERPRET A MAP

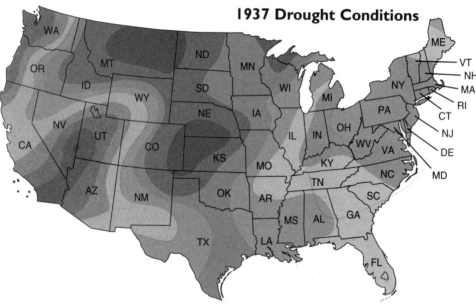

1937 Drought Conditions

rain below normal — rain above normal

−6 −4 −2 0 2 4 6

Great Plains States		
Colorado (CO)	Nebraska (NE)	South Dakota (SD)
Kansas (KS)	New Mexico (NM)	Texas (TX)
Minnesota (MN)	North Dakota (ND)	Wyoming (WY)
Montana (MT)	Oklahoma (OK)	

Farmers and crops suffered across the Great Plains in the 1930s. During a drought—a long period of time with little or no rain—crops cannot grow well. The map shows how bad the drought was in 1937. The key shows drought conditions on a scale from −6 to 6. A −6 stands for the driest conditions. A 6 stands for very wet conditions. Use the key to match the numbers to the shading on the map.

▶ *What were conditions like in Willa Cather's home state of Nebraska?*

_____

_____

▶ How did conditions in the Great Plains compare with conditions in other parts of the country?

_____

_____

▶ Propose Explanations

THINK ABOUT SOIL EROSION Each area has an amount of rainfall that is average, or typical, for that area. Some years bring heavier than average rainfall, while others are drier than average. Droughts are natural. The grasslands of the Great Plains had droughts before the settlers arrived from the east. And high winds are common in this mainly flat, treeless area. But these winds did not carry away soil until after the land was farmed.

Farmers replaced the thick tangles of native grasses with crops such as corn and wheat. After harvesting the crops, farmers left the fields unplanted. The few trees that did exist were removed so that farm equipment could move easily through the fields.

▶ *How did these farming practices contribute to soil erosion?*

_____

_____

_____

_____

_____

_____

_____

_____

▶ Take Action

WRITE A LETTER Imagine that your family moved to a farm on the Great Plains in 1928 when there was plenty of rain. It is now 1934 and three years into the drought.

▶ *On a separate sheet of paper, write a letter to a cousin on the East Coast. Describe how the land and farming has changed since your family arrived. Explain what you think your family will do next.*

Conserving Soil

Dust in the Wind

Dust storms blew many farmers out of town.

The drought of the 1930s was a disaster for many Great Plains farmers. The dry topsoil blew away in great dust storms. This dust gave the region and the disaster their unwelcome name—the Dust Bowl. As the drought wore on, many farm families packed up their belongings and left. About 350,000 people moved from the Great Plains to California between 1935 and 1939.

Woody Guthrie was a popular songwriter and folksinger of that time. He wrote several songs about the Dust Bowl.

▲ Dust Bowl refugees

Before You Read

USE YOUR IMAGINATION Imagine yourself outdoors as a dust storm approaches. It may help to think of a heavy, windy snowstorm, then imagine the snow as sand and dust. How would the sky look? How would farm animals react? How would you react? Write your ideas.

_____

_____

_____

_____

_____

_____

_____

_____

UNIT 2: DYNAMIC EARTH

 **Read**

NOTEZONE

Circle all the adjectives that describe how bad the dust storm was.

In this song, Woody Guthrie describes "Black Sunday," the worst storm of the Dust Bowl.

DUST STORM DISASTER

On the fourteenth day of April of nineteen thirty five
There struck the worst of dust storms that ever filled the sky.
You could see that dust storm coming the cloud looked death-like black
And through our mighty nation It left a dreadful track....

The storm took place at sundown. It lasted through the night.
When we looked out next morning We saw a terrible sight.
We saw outside our window Where wheatfields they had grown,
Was now a rippling ocean Of dust the wind had blown.

It covered up our fences, it covered up our barns,
It covered up our tractors In this wild and dusty storm.
We loaded our jalopies And piled our families in,
We rattled down the highway To never come back again.

----

jalopies: old, beat-up cars

From: Guthrie, Woody. "Dust Storm Disaster."
Ludlow Music, Inc.

◄ **Woody Guthrie**

FIND OUT MORE

SCIENCESAURUS

Weathering, Soil,
 and Erosion   188
Soil   191
Erosion
 and Deposition   192

SCI LINKS
THE WORLD'S A CLICK AWAY

www.scilinks.org
Keyword: Wind Erosion
Code: GSED07

MAKING INFERENCES

▶ *Where did the dust described in Woody Guthrie's song come from?*

_____

_____

▶ *What produced the "deathlike black cloud" Woody describes? (Hint: Look for clues later in the song.)*

_____

_____

Kansas: April 14, 1935

storm strikes
A huge dark cloud appears in the distance. A few minutes later the sky turns black. The cloud rolls over the land like a wave on the ocean. People have to crawl to find shelter.

storm over
The wind stops howling. The sky brightens. Outside, farmers find their animals dead or dying. Sand is piled in drifts against farm buildings. Farmers use shovels to uncover tractors. Much of the dried-out topsoil in their fields is gone.

The air temperature reaches 90°F (32°C). It's the hottest day so far this year.

8:00 A.M.   9:00   10:00   11:00   Noon   1:00 P.M.   2:00   3:00   4:00   5:00   6:00

The sky over the Great Plains is clear blue. After weeks of dust storms, no dust in the air today! Farm families hang their wash on clotheslines, expecting it will still be clean when it is dry.

The temperature is dropping rapidly. Wild birds are behaving strangely.

People in cars put on their headlights but still cannot see to drive, and crash. People at home stuff rags around their doors and windows to keep the dust out. It gets in anyway—in their noses, their mouths, and in their food.

▶ *Some people called this day "the day of the black blizzard." How was the dust storm like a severe snowstorm? How was it different?*

_____

_____

_____

_____

_____

58

THINK ABOUT IT Woody Guthrie wrote his song "Dust Bowl Disaster" about April 14, 1935.

▶ *What clues do the song and time line give that the dust storm on this day was only one of many?*

_____

_____

▶ *In what ways was this dust storm a disaster for the people who experienced it?*

_____

_____

▶ *According to the song, what did many farm families do after the "Black Sunday" dust storm? Why would they do this?*

_____

_____

_____

▶ Take Action

RESEARCH FOLK SONGS Woody Guthrie was one of many folksingers who wrote songs about the hardships of ordinary working people in the United States. Folk songs were one way that the stories of struggling people could be heard. Research songs by Guthrie and other songwriters of the 1930s. Find and listen to their recordings. What do their lyrics tell you about how most people lived? Give some examples of the songs and lyrics.

_____

_____

_____

_____

_____

_____

_____

_____

Conserving Soil

Saving the Land

North Americans learned many lessons from the Dust Bowl.

In 1900 the United States Bureau of Soils published a pamphlet about soil. It described soil as a resource that would always be available. At first, the hopeful farmers of the Great Plains agreed. But in the 1930s, wind eroded the soil from their sun-baked fields into giant dust clouds. It didn't take long for farmers to see that to save the Great Plains topsoil, they had to change their farming methods so they would conserve soil.

▲ **Dust Bowl farm in Texas**

▶ **Explore**

READING A TABLE In the 1930s, U.S. government officials started to announce ways to keep the rich soil of the Great Plains from being eroded by wind. Today wind is still a problem on the flat, dry Great Plains. Farmers use several methods to prevent soil erosion. Read about their methods in the table.

GREAT PLAINS SOIL CONSERVATION	
Method	**Description**
Conservation tillage	plowing less deeply into the soil
Stubble mulching	leaving the stems (stubble) and roots of crop plants in the soil after harvest
Cover crops	growing low, grass-like plants in harvested fields until it is time to plant the next crop
Strip cropping	planting strips of wind-resistant crops next to crops that do not resist the wind
Windbreaks	planting trees or hedges along the edges of fields
Restoring wild grasslands	stop planting crops on land that erodes; instead, replant it with wild grasses that grow in thick tangles

UNIT 2: DYNAMIC EARTH

Propose Explanations

RECOGNIZING CAUSE AND EFFECT Using the information in the table, explain how each of the six methods could prevent soil erosion by wind.

▶ *Conservation tillage*

_____

_____

▶ *Stubble mulching*

_____

_____

▶ *Cover crops*

_____

_____

▶ *Strip cropping*

_____

_____

▶ *Windbreaks*

_____

_____

▶ *Restoring wild grasslands*

_____

_____

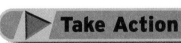

Take Action

DESIGN A PAMPHLET You have a chance to update the 1900 pamphlet from the Bureau of Soils. On a separate sheet of paper, design a new pamphlet for farmers. Stress the importance of soil conservation. Use both words and pictures to communicate your message. Design an eye-catching cover that communicates the main message of the pamphlet.

Changing Shorelines

Shifting Sands

What's attacking our beaches? The elements, my dear Watson.

If you've ever visited the ocean, you know that waves constantly pound the shore. On stormy days the waves are bigger and strike with greater force. On calm days the waves are smaller and strike with lesser force. But the pounding is constant. Erosion takes place when blowing wind or moving water carries away sediments such as sand and soil particles. Deposition takes place when wind and water drop those sediments in a new place. Erosion and deposition are constantly at work along our nation's shorelines. Some areas are built up while other areas are worn down.

▶ Before You Read

MAP YOUR IDEAS Shorelines make up less than 10 percent of Earth's land surface. Yet about 66 percent of the world's population lives along a coast.

▶ *Why do you think people want to live, work, and vacation close to the ocean? Organize your ideas by completing the idea map.*

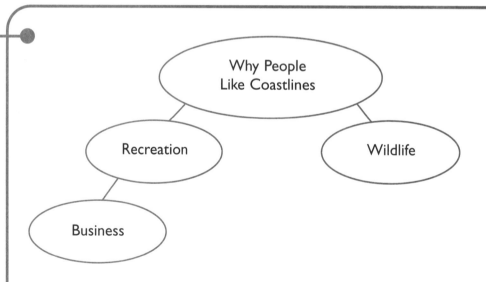

Why People Like Coastlines

Recreation

Wildlife

Business

▶ **Read**

Here's how erosion affects shorelines.

Beach Erosion

Erosion is...plaguing [America's shorelines]. Coastal residents up and down the United States are worrying about undermined cliffs, disappearing beaches, and the occasional dwelling diving into the briny.

Beaches are constantly moving, building up here and eroding there, in response to waves, winds, storms and relative sea level rise.... Hurricanes or [storms called] northeasters...cause the most dramatic damage to beaches.

...Barrier beaches...protect land from the sea [and are] vulnerable to obliteration by the very factor that makes [them] so glamorous: the sea.... And the problem is increasing because the sea is rising [at a faster rate] after centuries of relatively slow rise, and scientists anticipate that the rate of rise will continue to increase...[during this] century.

Still, erosion cuts in two directions, says Jim O'Connell, a coastal processes specialist with the Sea Grant program at Woods Hole Oceanographic Institution [in Massachusetts]. "Without the process of erosion, we would not have the beaches, dunes, barrier beaches, and the highly productive bays and estuaries that owe their very existence to the presence of barrier beaches."

---

undermined: gradually worn away from below
dwelling: house
briny: the ocean
barrier beach: a long, low, sandy beach attached to the mainland; the shallow water between a barrier beach and the mainland is called a lagoon

obliteration: total destruction
processes: actions and changes
estuary: an area where a river empties into the ocean and there is mixing of fresh water and salt water (See diagram on page 64.)

From: "Beach Erosion." *The Why Files.* University of Wisconsin. (whyfiles.org/091beach/)

FIND OUT MORE

SCIENCESAURUS
Erosion and
Deposition   192

SCi**LINKS**
THE WORLD'S A CLICK AWAY

www.scilinks.org
Keyword: Wave Erosion
Code: GSED08

CUTTING IN TWO DIRECTIONS

▶ *Find and label the barrier beaches in the diagram. Use the definition on page 63 to help you identify them.*

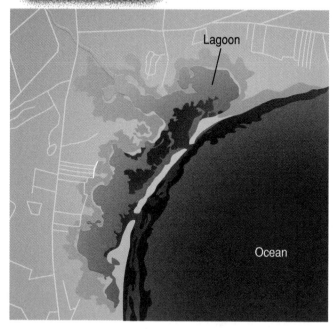

Jim O'Connell points out that while erosion *does* cut away at beaches, it is also the *source* of beach sand in the first place. Beaches are made up of sediments such as sand. Most beach sediments are carried to coastlines by rivers. The rivers deposit the sediments at the shore and on the ocean floor beyond the shore. Then wave action pushes most of the sediments onto the shoreline to build beaches. Waves also push sand along the shore.

▶ *Label the river in the diagram. Label where sediments are deposited by the river and by wave action. Draw arrows to show in which direction forces move the sediments.*

Jim O'Connell says without erosion there would be no beaches at all.

▶ *How does erosion contribute to making beaches?*

_____

_____

RECOGNIZING CAUSE AND EFFECT

▶ *What is it about beaches that makes them erode so easily? Think about both what they are made of and the forces they are exposed to.*

_____

_____

_____

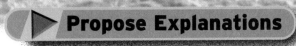

Propose Explanations

COMINGS AND GOINGS OF ISLAND PEOPLE Barrier beaches and barrier islands stretch along much of the eastern and Gulf coastlines of the U.S. A barrier island is like a barrier beach except it is not attached to the mainland. Many of these beaches and islands are covered with vacation homes, hotels, restaurants, and other buildings. Both beaches and islands are made mostly of loose sand. Wind, waves, and water currents move the sand. The sand is deposited on other parts of the island or dragged out to sea.

▶ *Label the barrier island in the diagram on page 64.*

How have people who live and work on these beaches and islands coped with erosion? One hundred years ago, when these areas had small populations, whole towns moved and rebuilt on the mainland. People who owned property along the ocean sometimes moved their houses and other structures back from the water. Over time, however, the number of people living in these places has grown. There are fewer places that people can move to when their houses are threatened by erosion.

▶ *Why might people today not want to move?*

_____

_____

_____

Take Action

ANALYZE THE ISSUE In 2000 the U.S. Congress asked scientists to report on erosion hazards. Their report said that 25 percent of homes and other structures within 500 feet (152 meters) of the U.S. coastline might be lost to erosion in the next 60 years. Should the government use taxes collected from everyone to help save homes built along the shoreline?

▶ *How might people who own beach houses answer the question?*

_____

_____

▶ *How might people who don't own beach houses answer?*

_____

_____

_____

_____

Changing Shorelines

Saving a Lighthouse

Sometimes, retreating is the best option.

For 200 years the Cape Hatteras Lighthouse stood on a North Carolina barrier island, warning ships away from dangerous waters. But over the years, erosion carried away much of the sand between the lighthouse and the Atlantic Ocean. By 1999 something had to be done if people wanted to save the lighthouse. The local community had to make some hard decisions. Scientists analyzed the patterns of erosion. Engineers proposed ways to protect the lighthouse.

 **Before You Read**

WHY WE NEED LIGHTHOUSES What is the purpose of a lighthouse? Explain what you know about lighthouses. You can use a drawing in your explanation.

FIND OUT MORE

SCIENCESAURUS
Erosion and
Deposition   192

▶ Read

NOTEZONE

What else
would you
like to know
about the
Cape Hatteras
Lighthouse?

After years of fighting beach erosion, there seemed only one good option left to save the Cape Hatteras Lighthouse.

A LIGHTHOUSE ON THE MOVE

22 JULY 1999

If you need some second-hand [moving] boxes, the Cape Hatteras Lighthouse is the place to look. After all, the 208-foot [63-meter] tall landmark was just hauled more than a quarter-mile [0.4 kilometers] back from its former perch, where it was threatened by the encroaching sea. And the end of every big move, we know, is signaled by a curbside littered with cardboard.

The lighthouse went a'truckin' after coastal erosion chewed away about 1,300 feet [400 meters] of beach, bringing the waves to within 150 feet [75 meters] of the 4,800-ton [4,877 metric ton] sentinel. When the...[lighthouse] was erected in 1870, it stood about 1,500 feet [460 meters] back from the waves.

The lighthouse, on the Outer Banks, North Carolina's long...[barrier islands], was built to warn ships from waters called "the graveyard of the Atlantic." The move should serve as a warning about the growing problem of coastal erosion.

- -

landmark: a distinctive feature of a landscape
hauled: moved by pulling or dragging

perch: a place to sit or rest
encroaching: moving in slowly
sentinel: guard
erected: put up

From: "Beach Erosion." *The Why Files.* University of Wisconsin. (whyfiles.org/091beach/)

The Cape Hatteras Lighthouse ▶

THE HISTORY OF THE LIGHTHOUSE The history of the lighthouse on Cape Hatteras, North Carolina, has been one long fight against the sea. The time line below shows actions taken over the years to protect the lighthouse from the effects of erosion.

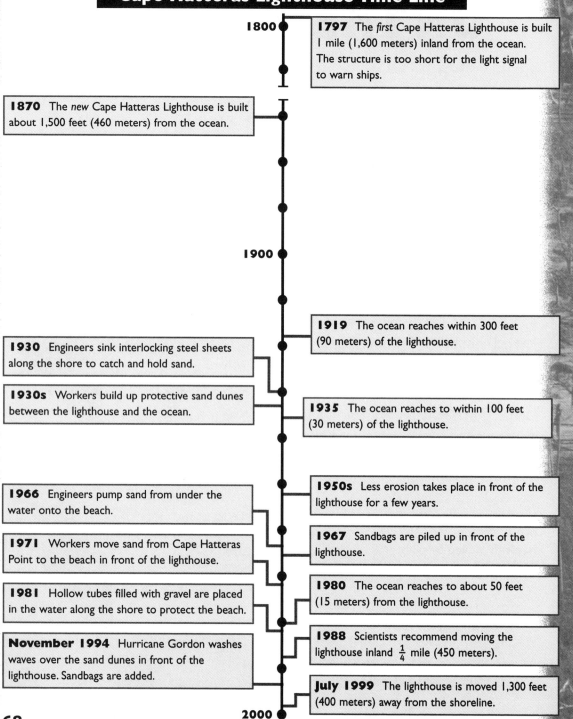

Cape Hatteras Lighthouse Time Line

1800

1797 The *first* Cape Hatteras Lighthouse is built 1 mile (1,600 meters) inland from the ocean. The structure is too short for the light signal to warn ships.

1870 The *new* Cape Hatteras Lighthouse is built about 1,500 feet (460 meters) from the ocean.

1900

1919 The ocean reaches within 300 feet (90 meters) of the lighthouse.

1930 Engineers sink interlocking steel sheets along the shore to catch and hold sand.

1930s Workers build up protective sand dunes between the lighthouse and the ocean.

1935 The ocean reaches to within 100 feet (30 meters) of the lighthouse.

1966 Engineers pump sand from under the water onto the beach.

1950s Less erosion takes place in front of the lighthouse for a few years.

1971 Workers move sand from Cape Hatteras Point to the beach in front of the lighthouse.

1967 Sandbags are piled up in front of the lighthouse.

1981 Hollow tubes filled with gravel are placed in the water along the shore to protect the beach.

1980 The ocean reaches to about 50 feet (15 meters) from the lighthouse.

November 1994 Hurricane Gordon washes waves over the sand dunes in front of the lighthouse. Sandbags are added.

1988 Scientists recommend moving the lighthouse inland $\frac{1}{4}$ mile (450 meters).

July 1999 The lighthouse is moved 1,300 feet (400 meters) away from the shoreline.

2000

THINK ABOUT IT

▶ *List the ways that people tried to prevent erosion of the beach around the lighthouse.*

_____

_____

_____

_____

_____

▶ *Why do you think the first lighthouse was built so far from the ocean?*

_____

_____

_____

_____

_____

▶ *Why do you think so many other solutions were tried before the lighthouse was moved in 1999?*

_____

_____

_____

_____

▶ **Take Action**

EXPLORING PROS AND CONS Think about all the ways engineers tried to reduce or repair the effects of erosion on Cape Hatteras. None of the methods worked for long. What would you say to a community trying to save its beach? List the arguments for and against fighting beach erosion. List the arguments for and against letting erosion take place. On a separate sheet of paper, summarize your ideas in a chart that presents both sides of the issue.

Changing Shorelines

Investigating Erosion

Hurricanes cause the most beach erosion.

When Hurricane Dennis struck the east coast of the U.S. in September 1999, it did a lot of damage. A hurricane's strong winds and powerful waves can change shorelines dramatically in a short period of time. Scientists are interested in what kinds of erosion damage are done by hurricanes. They hope to use the information to save properties and lives in future storms.

 **Read**

NOTEZONE

When did Hurricane Dennis strike North Carolina's coast?

When was the Cape Hatteras Lighthouse moved?

What do you notice about these dates?

When a hurricane strikes, erosion scientists move in to check the damage.

EYE-POPPING EROSION

10 September 1999

[Hurricane] Dennis...teased the Atlantic coast with whipping winds and battering waves before finally making landfall on Saturday.... [Dennis] caused "eye-popping erosion" and...the worst scouring of North Carolina's coast in 20 years. This week, teams of USGS scientists are on the ground, making measurements of the eroded beaches.... [The scientists are also] flying over the coastline to take video and still photographs of the damage caused by Dennis....

The data collected this week will be compared with data collected before and after other hurricanes and coastal storms.... [This will help scientists] track long-term changes to the coastline.... [It will also help them understand] the effects of storms on beaches, protective dunes, and the topography of the region. These changes... reflect the hazards to life and property during a major coastal storm.

"Ultimately, we want to be able to provide sound, scientific data to local officials and builders.... [They] can then decide how far back structures should be set or where they shouldn't be set at all," said [USGS oceanographer and coastal erosion expert Abby] Sallenger.

making landfall: reaching land
scouring: forceful scrubbing
USGS: United States Geological Survey, a government life and earth science agency

topography: features of the land surface
oceanographer: a scientist who studies the ocean

From: "Dennis Dissipates, Work Just Begins for USGS Scientists." *United States Geological Survey.*
U.S. Department of the Interior.
(www.usgs.gov/public/press/public_affairs/press_releases/pr979m.html)

 **Explore**

BEFORE AND AFTER This photo was taken by the USGS team after Hurricane Dennis. The X marks the position of the lighthouse before it was moved. You can see the lighthouse's straight pathway through the sand dunes when it was moved.

▶ *What might have happened if the lighthouse had not been moved before the hurricane? What details in the photo support your answer?*

_____

_____

_____

▶ *How can people use what the scientists learned about coastline erosion during storms? Think about risks to both life and property.*

_____

_____

_____

The Puzzle of Earth's Crust

Fitting the Continents Together

In science, new ideas are accepted only when there is evidence to support them.

Alfred Wegener was trained as an astronomer and worked as a meteorologist. A meteorologist is a scientist who studies weather. But what made Wegener famous were his ideas about geology. Geology is the study of Earth's processes, structure, composition, and history. In the early 1900s, geologists thought that the continents had always been where they are today. Wegener studied reports of similar fossils and rocks found on continents separated by the ocean. He hypothesized that today's continents were at one time joined as one giant continent. He explained that slowly, the giant continent had broken apart. Over 200 million years, the pieces drifted to where they are found today. Wegener's idea—called *continental drift*—was revolutionary. And it was not very popular with other scientists.

Africa

South
America

► **Before You Read**

WHAT WOULD YOU DO? Imagine you are at a scientific meeting of geologists. Someone stands up and says, "My name is Alfred Wegener and I am a meteorologist. Let me tell you my great new idea about Earth's history. It's based on evidence from fossils and rocks found on different continents."

► *Would you be willing to listen to Wegener? Explain your answer.*

_____

_____

_____

_____

_____

_____

_____

_____

_____

▶ Read

NOTEZONE

Underline the clue that started Wegener thinking about Earth's continents.

How many scientists other than Wegener are quoted?

Geologists were shocked when Alfred Wegener presented his idea of drifting continents.

A Revolutionary Idea

"Doesn't the east coast of South America fit exactly against the west coast of Africa, as if they had once been joined?" wrote Wegener to his future wife in December 1910. "This is an idea I'll have to pursue."

...Just a [year] later, on January 6, 1912, Wegener startled a meeting of the Geological Association in Frankfurt, [Germany] with his radical theory...a grand vision of drifting continents and widening seas to explain the evolution of Earth's geography.

"Utter, damned rot!" said the president of the prestigious American Philosophical Society.

"If we are to believe [this theory], we must forget everything we have learned in the last 70 years and start all over again," said another American scientist.

Anyone who "valued his reputation for scientific sanity" would never dare support such a theory, said a British geologist.

Thus did most in the scientific community ridicule the concept that would revolutionize the earth sciences and revile the man who dared to propose it, German meteorological pioneer and polar explorer Alfred Wegener.

◄ **Dr. Alfred Wegener**

radical: very different from the usual

theory: an idea that explains how many scientific observations are related

geography: the study of Earth's features, climates, and conditions that affect people

prestigious: well-respected

ridicule: make fun of

revile: verbally attack

From: Hughes, Patrick. "The Meteorologist Who Started a Revolution." *Weatherwise.*

FIND OUT MORE

SCIENCESAURUS

Plate Tectonics and Mountain Building 181
Continental Drift 182

SciLINKS
THE WORLD'S A CLICK AWAY

www.scilinks.org
Keyword: Continental Drift
Code: GSED09

73

 **Explore**

COMPARING THEORIES Wegener spent most of 1911 studying the work of geologists. He read about identical fossils found in South America and Africa. The fossils showed that the same kinds of animals lived on the two continents at the same time. Most geologists thought it was impossible for continents to move. Even Wegener could not explain how it happened. Some geologists hypothesized that long land bridges must have connected the two continents. They believed that over time, these bridges had sunk into the ocean so they could no longer be seen.

▶ *How did Wegener explain why the fossils matched?*

_____

_____

Wegener researched the work of other geologists. He read that rock formations on the east coast of South America and the west coast of Africa matched.

▶ *How did Wegener's theory explain these matching rock formations?*

_____

_____

_____

▶ *How might the land bridge hypothesis explain the same fossils and rock formations?*

_____

_____

▶ *Why do you think the scientists at the Geological Association meeting rejected Wegener's theory of continental drift?*

_____

_____

_____

_____

_____

_____

74

AN ADVENTUROUS SCIENTIST As a boy, Wegener dreamed of exploring the Arctic. He was excited by the challenge of exploring and making new discoveries. As an adult scientist he was also adventurous. He tested a new weather instrument in a long hot-air balloon flight. He survived the longest crossing of an ice sheet ever made. (An ice sheet is a huge, thick glacier covering a large land area.) In fact, Wegener died on the Arctic ice after trying to save other men.

▶ *Someone who is adventurous is willing to take chances. What kinds of chances did Wegener take as an explorer?*

_____

_____

▶ *What kinds of chances did Wegener take as a thinker?*

_____

_____

Wegener did not give up on his theory of continental drift. He continued to work on it for the rest of his life. It was another 50 years before other scientists accepted the idea that continents could be moving.

▶ Take Action

IT'S FUNNY—BUT IS IT SCIENCE?

▶ *This cartoon is funny because it doesn't represent continental drift accurately. Explain why the cartoon and caption are not accurate.*

_____

_____

_____

_____

_____

_____

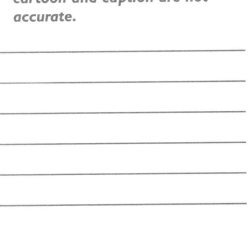

FERRY RIDES FROM AFRICA TO SOUTH AMERICA — 2 CLAMS —

Continental drift would eventually force Og to raise his rates.

The Puzzle of Earth's Crust

EXPLAINING HOW CONTINENTS MOVE

While at sea with the U.S. Navy, Harry Hess found time to do scientific research.

Harry Hess was a geologist at Princeton University. He was also a ship commander in the United States Navy. During World War II, Hess was at sea on a navy ship. Crossing back and forth across the oceans gave Hess the chance to collect data about the ocean floor.

After the war, geologists continued to collect data. During the late 1940s and 1950s, the first complete map of the ocean floor was put together. Hess studied the map and had an idea that could explain how continents move.

▶ **Read**

Here's how Harry Hess came up with his idea.

Underwater Clues

Between military missions, Hess's thoughts often turned to geology. Like most ships of its class, the *Cape Johnson* was equipped with an echo sounder…. [The echo sounder sent] out pulses of sound that bounced off the ocean floor. [Then it] measured the time for [the pulses] to return,…calculating the water's depth. As Hess voyaged around the globe in this ship,…the steady ping of the echo sounder generated a profile of the ocean floor….

In 1960 [Hess] attempted to explain…[these] observations of the ocean floor [and his theory about seafloor spreading]…. A brilliant scientist, Hess was… perhaps tentative about the new ideas he was presenting. In his introduction [to a scientific report] he adopted a cautious tone. "I shall consider this paper an essay in geopoetry," he wrote, hinting that his colleagues should keep an open mind about his conclusions.

...More than geopoetry, Hess's theory of seafloor spreading was the key to the earth's behavior. But most of his contemporaries didn't see it that way. At the time, the geological community, particularly in the United States, still believed strongly in an earth with an immovable crust. They greeted Hess's ideas with skepticism or outright disdain.

▲ **Harry Hess**

generated: produced
profile: a view from the side
tentative: unsure
geopoetry: poetry about geology
colleague: a member of the same profession

contemporary: a person living at the same time
skepticism: disbelief
disdain: dislike, scorn

From: Vogel, Shawna. *Naked Earth: The New Geophysics.* Dutton, a division of Penguin Putnam, Inc.

▶ **Explore**

INTERPRETING A DIAGRAM The diagram below shows how an echo sounder works. As the ship moves forward, the transmitter sends sound signals down to the ocean floor. The signals bounce back to the receiver. The length of time it takes for a signal to bounce back shows how deep the ocean floor is at that point. Where the ocean floor is deeper, the signal takes longer to bounce back. Where the ocean floor is shallower, the signal bounces back more quickly. All the "bounce-back" times are plotted on a graph. Connecting the points with a line creates a profile of the ocean floor.

▶ *If the line on the graph suddenly went up and then down again, what would that tell you about that area of the ocean floor?*

_____

_____

_____

▶ *What kind of feature would you expect to see there on the ocean floor?*

_____

_____

_____

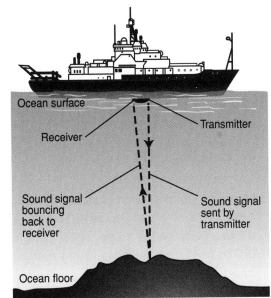

Ocean surface

Receiver

Transmitter

Sound signal bouncing back to receiver

Sound signal sent by transmitter

Ocean floor

HESS'S NEW THEORY The echo sounding profiles collected by Hess and others showed at least one mountain ridge in every ocean. New magma, hot melted rock, flowed out of each ridge. The profiles also showed deep trenches along the edges of the oceans. Hess hypothesized that new crust formed from the magma flowing out of the ridge. He also hypothesized that older crust was destroyed at the trenches. In this way Earth's crust was always moving. Hess's theory was called *seafloor spreading*.

▶ *Label the diagram to show where new crust forms. Label where old crust is destroyed.*

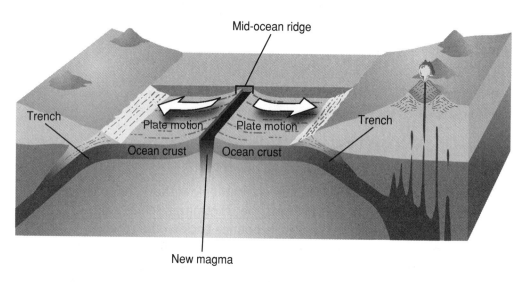

Mid-ocean ridge

Trench

Plate motion

Plate motion

Trench

Ocean crust

Ocean crust

New magma

▶ Propose Explanations

MAGNETIC EVIDENCE Hess developed a theory to explain how Earth's crust could move. A few years later, geologists discovered new evidence that supported Hess's theory. They found that the crust on both sides of a ridge has a pattern of magnetized bands. The magnetized minerals in the bands line up with Earth's magnetic poles, just like a compass needle does. In some bands, the magnetic pole in the minerals that should point north, does point north. In other bands, that same magnetic pole in the minerals points south.

Geologists already knew that Earth's magnetic poles have switched places many times over millions of years. They concluded that as bands of new crust formed at an ocean ridge, the minerals in the bands lined up with Earth's magnetic poles. When Earth's magnetic poles reversed, the magnetic poles in new bands of crust also reversed. This produced alternating magnetized bands on each side of the ridge. Then came the most important part of the new discovery. The geologists found *matching pairs* of magnetized bands on opposite sides of the ridge!

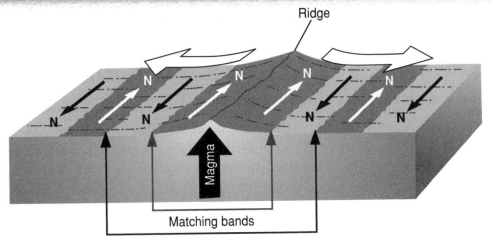

Ridge

Magma

Matching bands

▶ *How did this new evidence support Hess's theory of seafloor spreading?*

_____

_____

_____

_____

LINKING TWO THEORIES As you learned in Lesson 19, Alfred Wegener presented his theory of continental drift in 1912. Wegener said that over millions of years, the continents had slowly drifted to their present locations. But Wegener could not explain *how* continents could move. In the 1960s, Harry Hess's theory of seafloor spreading explained how Earth's crust moved. Because the continents sit on pieces of crust, they are carried along, too.

▶ *How did Hess's theory of seafloor spreading support Wegener's earlier ideas? How did this new evidence make it easier for scientists to accept the idea that continents are moving?*

_____

_____

_____

▶ *What would have happened to Wegener's theory if no one had found evidence that helped explain how continents could move?*

_____

_____

_____

The Puzzle of Earth's Crust

Using New Technology

With satellites, we can watch Earth move.

Both Alfred Wegener and Harry Hess made inferences about events they could not see. In recent years, scientists have used new technologies to gather evidence to test Wegener's and Hess's theories. One such technology is the Global Positioning System (GPS). GPS uses space satellites to identify the exact locations of points on Earth's surface.

NOTEZONE

Jot down a question about this to ask your teacher.

FIND OUT MORE

SCIENCESAURUS

▶ **Read**

Here's what scientists learned by using the Global Positioning System.

A MOVABLE CRUST

The most promising addition to [scientists'] toolbox is the Global Positioning System.... Geophysicists have been using...[GPS] to track crustal movements.... Hundreds of sites across the globe are continuously being monitored for their relative positions. And nothing emerges more clearly from these observations than the...[wandering] nature of our crust. A site in Sussex, England, is drifting away from one in Greenbelt, Maryland, at the rate of about two thirds of an inch [1.7 cm] a year. On the other side of the globe, two sites in Monument Park, California, and Simosato, Japan, are slowly converging.

geophysicist: a scientist who studies matter and forces related to geology

converging: coming together

From: Vogel, Shawna. *Naked Earth: The New Geophysics.* Dutton, a division of Penguin Putnam, Inc.

Explore

NEW EVIDENCE

▶ *What do geophysicists measure with GPS technology? What can they figure out from these measurements?*

_____

_____

_____

_____

_____

▶ *How do the data from GPS measurements support the theories of Wegener and Hess?*

_____

_____

Recently scientists measured the age of rocks near ridges and trenches. Hess said crust is made along a ridge and destroyed at the trenches.

▶ *Where does Hess's theory predict that the youngest rocks would be found?*

_____

Take Action

PLAN AN EXPEDITION You have been awarded the use of the deep-sea submersible *Alvin* for a scientific expedition. *Alvin* has a camera for taking pictures, robotic arms that can be used to pick up objects, and a sled to hold equipment for experiments.

▼ *Alvin*

You have eight hours to explore an ocean ridge or trench. It takes about two hours to reach the ocean floor and another two hours to return to the surface. On a separate sheet of paper, describe how you will use the remaining time for exploring, collecting, and experimenting. Be sure to tell whether you'll explore a ridge or a trench.

Volcanoes

The Pressure Builds

A volcano such as Mount St. Helens contains extremely hot gases and thick, sticky magma— an explosive combination.

Think about what happens when you shake a can of soda and then pop the top. Believe it or not, soda and magma—the molten rock inside a volcano—have something in common. Both liquids are full of gases. And when a gas under pressure is released, it can pack a lot of power.

▲ **Mount St. Helens after its 1980 eruption**

▶ **Before You Read**

BURSTING FORTH If you shake a can of soda, gas escapes from the liquid into the space at the top of the can. When you open the top, the pressure is suddenly released and the gas escapes. This is one example of pressure building and then releasing.

▶ *Describe other common examples of pressure building up and then being released. What happens when the pressure is released?*

_____

_____

_____

_____

_____

_____

_____

_____

UNIT 2: DYNAMIC EARTH

► Read

NOTEZONE

(Circle) each substance that can erupt from a volcano.

Beneath a volcano's surface, pressure is mounting.

HOW DO VOLCANOES ERUPT?

Some volcanic eruptions are explosive and others are not. How explosive an eruption is depends on how runny or sticky the magma is. If magma is thin and runny, gases can escape easily from it. When this type of magma erupts, it flows out of the volcano. Lava flows rarely kill people because they move slowly enough for people to get out of their way. Lava flows, however, can cause considerable destruction to buildings in their path. If magma is thick and sticky, gases cannot escape easily. Pressure builds up until the gases escape violently and explode…. They can blast out clouds of hot…[rocks] from the side or top of a volcano.

From: "How Do Volcanoes Erupt?" *USGS Cascades Volcano Observatory*. U.S. Department of the Interior. (vulcan.wr.usgs.gov/Outreach/AboutVolcanoes/ how_do_volcanoes_erupt.html)

FIND OUT MORE

SCIENCESAURUS

Minerals	179
Mountain Building and Volcanoes	187

SCi LINKS.
THE WORLD'S A CLICK AWAY

www.scilinks.org
Keyword: Volcanic Eruptions
Code: GSED10

▲ Mauna Ely in Hawaii

 **Activity**

STUCK INSIDE

Have you ever tried blowing bubbles into thick syrup?

What You Need:
- two small paper cups (6-ounce or larger)
- two straws
- 50 mL water
- 50 mL thick sugar syrup, such as corn syrup

What to Do:
1. Pour the water into one cup and the syrup into the other cup.
2. Put a straw in each cup.
3. Blow into each straw with one short breath.

What Do You See?
▶ *Describe what happened when you blew into each straw.*

When I blew into the straw in the water...	When I blew into the straw in the syrup...

Propose Explanations

WHAT'S THE DIFFERENCE? Think about your observations with the water and syrup.

▶ *What can you conclude about the difference between how a gas moves through thinner liquids and how it moves through thicker liquids?*

_____

_____

_____

_____

_____

▶ *What do your observations tell you about why thicker magma makes an eruption more explosive than thinner magma does?*

_____

_____

_____

_____

_____

The thickness of the magma inside a volcano depends on two things. The first is temperature. All magma is extremely hot (about 1,000°C). But hotter magma is thinner and runnier than slightly cooler magma. The mineral ingredients in the magma also affect its thickness. Different mineral ingredients have different properties. For example, silica—an important part of many solid minerals—makes magma syrupy thick when it is a liquid. As a result, magma that contains a lot of silica is very thick and sticky.

▶ *Would you expect the lava from an explosive eruption to have more silica or less silica than the lava from a quieter eruption? Explain.*

_____

_____

_____

_____

_____

Volcanoes

▼ **Goma resident watching lava flowing after Mount Nyiragongo erupted**

Rivers of Fire

The most dangerous kind of volcanic eruption quickly destroys everything in its path.

Volcanoes erupt in different ways at different times. Some eruptions produce a lava flow. This happened in January 2002, when Mount Nyiragongo in the Democratic Republic of Congo erupted. Red-hot lava flowed through the city of Goma. The homes of more than 12,000 families were destroyed.

Other eruptions are explosive, throwing a mixture of hot ash, rocks, and gases high into the air. Sometimes a gas-rock mixture behaves more like a liquid and flows downhill. This is called a *pyroclastic flow*.

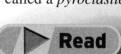 **Read**

NOTEZONE

What questions do you have after reading this?

FIND OUT MORE

SCIENCESAURUS

Mountain Building
and Volcanoes   187

SCiLINKS
THE WORLD'S A CLICK AWAY

www.scilinks.org
Keyword: Volcanic
Eruptions
Code: GSED10

A pyroclastic flow took place when Mount Pelée on the island of Martinique erupted in 1902.

St. Pierre Entirely Wiped Out

At about 7:50 A.M. on May 8, the volcano erupted with a deafening roar. A large black cloud composed of superheated gas, ash and rock rolled headlong down the south flank of Mt. Pelée at more than 100 miles [160 km] per hour.... In less than one minute it struck St. Pierre with hurricane force. The blast was powerful enough to carry a three-ton statue sixteen meters from its mount....The searing heat of the cloud ignited huge bonfires....The cloud continued to advance over the harbor where it destroyed at least twenty ships anchored offshore. The...blast capsized the steamship *Grappler*, and its scorching heat set ablaze the American sailing ship *Roraima*, killing most of her passengers and crew.... Of the...[almost] 28,000 people in St. Pierre, there were only two known survivors.

superheated: heated excessively   **ignited:** caught fire
flank: side or slope   **capsized:** turned over

From: Camp, Dr. Vic. "Mt. Pelée Eruption (1902)." *How Volcanoes Work*. Department of Geological Sciences, San Diego State University. (www.geology.sdsu.edu/how_volcanoes_work/Pelee.html)

▶ Explore

DIFFERENT FLOWS This table compares some properties of lava and pyroclastic flows. Use the information to answer the questions below.

	LAVA FLOW	PYROCLASTIC FLOW
Materials	molten rock with small gas bubbles	a cloud of gases containing rock particles
Density	quite dense	low density but dense enough to flow along the ground
Speed of flow	1–30 kilometers per hour	160–260 kilometers per hour
Temperature	700°–1,200°C	600°–700°C
Effect on ocean	sinks below ocean water while heating it	flows over ocean's surface

▶ *What do a pyroclastic flow and a lava flow have in common?*

_____

_____

▶ *Why does a pyroclastic flow travel more quickly than a lava flow?*

_____

_____

▶ *Do you think people can escape from a lava flow? Explain.*

_____

▶ *Do you think people can escape from a pyroclastic flow? Explain.*

_____

▶ *How could the pyroclastic flow from Mt. Pelée capsize and burn boats in the harbor? Could a lava flow cause the same destruction?*

_____

_____

_____

_____

_____

Volcanoes

Can Eruptions Be Predicted?

Volcanologists are working on the answer.

A volcanologist is a scientist who studies volcanoes. Volcanologists investigate the structure of volcanoes. They also study how volcanoes form rocks and change the atmosphere. Some volcanologists investigate ways to predict eruptions. Making accurate predictions is difficult. All the changes leading to an eruption take place below Earth's surface. Yet all the tests that scientists do take place on or above Earth's surface. Predictions about volcanoes are not yet reliable, but scientists keep observing and improving their techniques.

Before You Read

WHAT DO YOU THINK? Volcanic eruptions release molten lava, gases, rock particles, and ash onto Earth's surface and into the atmosphere.

▶ *What signs might there be that a volcano is about to erupt? Draw a diagram and write your ideas.*

UNIT 2: DYNAMIC EARTH

NOTEZONE

Circle all the clues used to predict volcano eruptions.

▶ Read

Here's how Chuck Wood, a volcanologist, answered a question about predicting volcanoes.

ASK A VOLCANOLOGIST

Question: Which method of predicting a volcanic eruption is the most useful and reliable?

Answer: Meaningful prediction requires careful monitoring of a volcano's vital signs. Seismometers can be used to pinpoint earthquakes which [follow] the rise of magma and its movement along fissures. Measurements of the tilt of the entire mountain provide additional information about the "breathing" of the volcano as magma moves inside it. Instruments that sniff...[sulfur dioxide, carbon dioxide] and other gases also can signal changes in the volcano. At some volcanoes the seismic information seems most reliable, at others the tilt tells the story. But the best predictions come from the combination of all of these methods into a volcano monitoring and prediction system.

And you must remember that each volcano is unique. The pattern of events that signifies an eruption at one volcano may not occur before an eruption at a different volcano. And the same volcano may change its eruptive behavior at any time! The good news is that general trends...are being observed at a variety of volcanoes around the world so that volcanologists are getting better at predicting eruptions.

monitoring: watching
vital signs: signs of life
seismometer: a device that senses earthquake motion
fissure: a fracture or crack in Earth's crust

seismic: related to an earthquake
signifies: is a sign of
trend: a change over time

From: Wood, Chuck. "Which Method Of Volcano Prediction Is The Most Useful And Reliable?." *Volcano World.* University of North Dakota.
(volcano.und.nodak.edu/vwdocs/frequent_questions/grp3/question229.html)

FIND OUT MORE

SCIENCESAURUS

Earthquakes   186
Mountain Building
  and Volcanoes   187

SCiLINKS.
THE WORLD'S A CLICK AWAY

www.scilinks.org
Keyword: Volcanic
  Eruptions
Code: GSED10

PREDICTING ON PINATUBO

PREDICTING ON PINATUBO On May 13, 1991, scientists measured 500 tons of sulfur dioxide coming out of Mt. Pinatubo in the Philippines. Two weeks later, scientists measured 5,000 tons. On June 12, 1991, Pinatubo erupted.

▶ *How many times greater than the May 13 release was the release measured two weeks later?*

_____

An increase in the release of sulfur dioxide gas is evidence that magma is moving toward the surface.

▶ *What could scientists predict about Pinatubo when they took the second measurement?*

_____

_____

The first sign of activity on Pinatubo had been a cloud of steam on April 2, 1991. A team of scientists from the United States recommended that people living nearby be evacuated. In all, 100,000 people moved away from their homes. If they hadn't, thousands of lives would have been lost in the eruption on June 12.

Two factors help volcanologists predict eruptions more successfully. The first is knowing the volcano's history of eruptions. The second is establishing a permanent station on the volcano. These stations make observations 24 hours a day, year-round.

▶ *How can each of these factors make scientists' predictions more accurate?*

_____

_____

_____

_____

_____

PREDICTING RISK Volcanologists are getting better at predicting when an eruption will take place. But they also want to predict how bad the eruption will be. They want to be able to predict the risk to people, crops, livestock, and structures. For example, there is an active volcano on Montserrat Island in the Caribbean Sea. Volcanologists have been monitoring the eruptions that began there in 1995. Since then, there have been lava flows, pyroclastic flows, and ash clouds.

Volcanologists recommended creating an exclusion zone on Montserrat where only scientists and others with government permission may go.

▶ *Why would most people be kept out of an exclusion zone? What risk might there be in that area?*

_____

_____

_____

Volcanologists compared their data from Montserrat with data from similar volcanoes around the world. They found that if an eruption has been going on for 80 months or longer, then it can be expected to last at least 20 years.

▶ *If Monseratt erupted from July 1995 to March 2002, should scientists predict it will erupt for 20 years? Explain.*

_____

_____

_____

▶ **Take Action**

ASKING QUESTIONS There are 1,300 active volcanoes around the world. Half a billion people live close to them.

▶ *Make a list of questions you'd want scientists to answer in order to decide how dangerous it is to be near a particular volcano.*

_____

_____

_____

_____

_____

_____

_____

_____

_____

_____

UNIT 3 Water on Earth

Earth has its own water recycling system.

If you've ever been caught in a downpour, you might have wondered where so much water could come from. Rain doesn't fall from outer space. All water on Earth is found on or below Earth's surface or in the air above us. Water molecules simply move from one place to another.

In this unit you'll learn about Earth's water. You'll examine the water cycle—the continuous movement of water between Earth's surface and the atmosphere. You'll find out what was done to a river in western Massachusetts to provide a water supply for the city of Boston. You'll explore creative ways to obtain water in dry areas—catching fog, removing the salt from ocean water, and towing icebergs. And you'll find out how ocean water can be used to generate electricity.

? Did You Know?
The Iguassu Falls in Brazil are made up of 275 waterfalls and are about as wide as 36 football fields! An average of 1.2 million cubic meters (42.4 million cubic feet) of water falls every second.

93

The Water Cycle

Round and Round It Goes

Like a merry-go-round, water is always on the move.

Water to drink, to cook our food, to shower in, to grow plants to eat, to keep cool—it's necessary for life. How often do you think about where your water comes from?

 **Explore**

FOLLOW THE WATER There's only so much water on Earth. It just gets recycled—naturally. Trace the movement of water on the diagram.

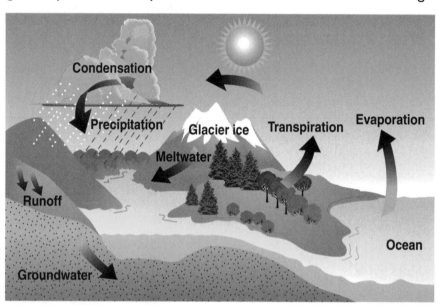

condensation: the process in which a gas changes to a liquid

precipitation: liquid or frozen water falling from clouds

runoff: water that flows over the ground surface

groundwater: water that collects below the ground surface

transpiration: the process in which plants give off water vapor through their leaves

evaporation: the process in which a liquid changes to a gas

glacier: a large mass of ice

meltwater: water melting from a glacier

Ocean water contains many dissolved minerals. This makes the ocean salty. Land organisms cannot use salty water. They need fresh water—water with much less dissolved salts.

▶ *Find all the places on the water cycle diagram that have fresh water. Mark these parts of the diagram "FW."*

▶ Activity

WATER, WATER, EVERYWHERE

A particle of water can end up anywhere in the water cycle. Toss a water cycle cube and see for yourself.

What You Need:
- full-size cube diagram
- sheet of paper
- pencil
- scissors
- clear tape

What To Do:
1. Your teacher will give you a full-size copy of the cube diagram on this page. DO NOT CUT THIS BOOK.
2. Cut along the solid lines.
3. Fold on the dotted lines.
4. Tape the squares together to make a cube.
5. Toss the cube four times. Read the label shown on the top side of the cube each time. On the sheet of paper, list the labels in the order they appear. If you get any label twice, toss again.

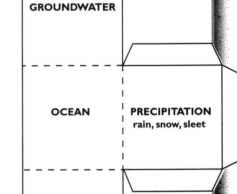

GROUNDWATER

OCEAN

PRECIPITATION
rain, snow, sleet

SURFACE
WATER
lake, river,
pond, stream

ATMOSPHERE
clouds (water or
ice), water vapor

GLACIER

WHAT DO YOU SEE? Describe how water moves from the first place on your list to the second. Identify the changes that the water goes through to get there and what makes those changes happen. (The water may go through more than one step to get from the first place to the second.) Then explain how the water gets from the second place to the third and from the third to the fourth.

_____

_____

_____

_____

FIND OUT MORE

SCIENCESAURUS

Water Cycle	216
Clouds	223
States of Matter	253
Changing States of Matter	255

SCI LINKS.
THE WORLD'S A CLICK AWAY

www.scilinks.org
Keyword: Water Cycle
Code: GSED11

The Water Cycle

Fog Catchers

Bolivia

Paragua

Chungungo,
Chile

Argentina

Uruguay

How do you collect fresh water from fog?

The fishing village of Chungungo sits on Chile's dry northern coast. Although the seacoast is often foggy, the area gets little rain. The villagers were always in need of fresh water. A team of scientists from Chile and Canada thought about the problem. They knew that for thousands of years, people around the world collected fog water that got caught in trees and ran down the trunks. The scientists planned a new twist on this old idea to obtain fresh water for the village.

Professor Pilar Cereceda is a member of the team. She has visited Chungungo many times to work with the villagers on the water project.

 **Before You Read**

MAKE A CONCEPT WEB Have you ever been in fog or seen a picture of it? What time of day was it? How did it look? How far could you see? How did it feel? What did it remind you of? Complete this concept web to organize your ideas.

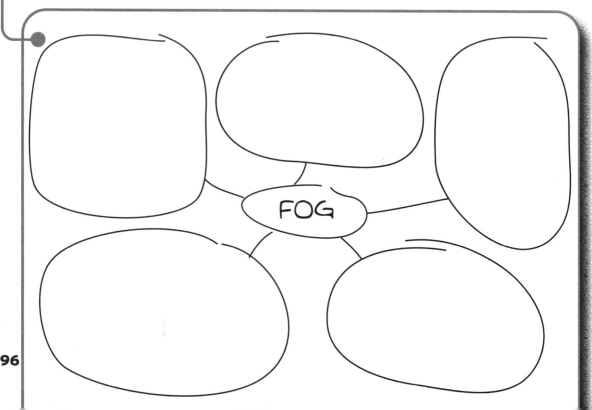

FOG

UNIT 3: WATER ON EARTH

▶ Read

NOTEZONE

Underline the words or phrases that describe the fog catchers.

Here's how Professor Cereceda helped make a big difference for a small village.

Collecting Fog

Returning to the tiny seaside village of Chungungo (population 330) in northern Chile is quite often an emotional experience for Pilar Cereceda, researcher and geography professor at the University of Chile in Santiago.

Fourteen years ago, when Cereceda first arrived to begin her research project, Chungungo was just one of hundreds of villages in the region that had no local source of fresh water…. The "miracle" of clean fresh water…came about through the introduction of large fog collectors: "a kind of volleyball net, which captures the fog (called camanchaca), typical of northern Chile," explains Cereceda….

The process involves the installation of polypropylene mesh nets, 12 meters [39 feet] long and 4 meters [13 feet] high, situated high in the mountains above the village. Fog, which is a regular phenomenon in the area, passes through the mesh and leaves behind droplets that trickle down to a trough that carries the water to a storage tank in the village.

"I still remember the day the village of Chungungo inaugurated the water system. This is something they never, ever thought would come to their village," recalls Cereceda.

▼ Fog collectors

FIND OUT MORE

SCIENCESAURUS
Water Cycle   216
Clouds   223
Steps in
  Technology
  Design   357

SCILINKS®
THE WORLD'S A CLICK AWAY
www.scilinks.org
Keyword: Clouds and Fog
Code: GSED12

---

fog: a cloud close to the ground
installation: setting up
polypropylene: a type of plastic

phenomenon: an event that can be observed
trough: a long, shallow channel
inaugurated: formally began

From: de Luigi, Maria. "Pilar Cereceda (Chile)." *In Person.* International Development Research Centre. (www.idrc.ca/library/document/102386/cereceda.html))

Explore

A FOGGY SOURCE Chungungo is very dry because of its location on Chile's northern coast. To the east, the high Andes Mountains block moist air from reaching the coast. To the west, cold-flowing ocean waters help to keep the air stable and prevent rain clouds from forming.

Use the diagram of the water cycle on page 94 and the information in this lesson to answer this question.

▶ *Fog forms when water vapor condenses into droplets of water in the air. What was the source of the water vapor in the fog?*

_____

_____

_____

SHOW HOW IT WORKS Review the description of the fog collection system in the reading. Draw and label a diagram showing the seacoast with fog moving in, the village of Chungungo, the mountains, and the fog collectors. Show how the water gets from the collectors to the village.

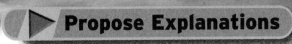
BEEN THERE, DONE THAT Before the team designed their system to collect fog, they read what other scientists had done. They found that 30 years before, another Chilean scientist had built nets to catch fog. Professor Cereceda spoke with the scientist. He told her about the work of scientists in other countries that he had read about.

▶ *How do you think the work of other scientists might have helped Professor Cereceda in her work?*

_____

_____

_____

_____

_____

Professor Cereceda says that science research should be used to improve people's lives. Before the villagers built the fog collection system, they had as little as one liter of fresh water per person each day—just enough to drink. Afterwards, they had about 30 liters per person each day.

▶ *Think of the ways you use water. Then list ways that the villagers might be using the additional water. How would having more fresh water improve the villagers' lives?*

_____

_____

_____

_____

_____

Take Action

DESIGN A FLYER Chungungo was just one of hundreds of villages in need of fresh water. On a separate sheet of paper, design a flyer to hand out to the people in other villages. Explain that villagers and scientists can work together to build a fog collection system. Briefly tell and show how the system works. Describe the benefits of the system. Include reports from villagers in Chungungo, telling how the system has helped them.

The Water Cycle

To Fog or Not To Fog

Where can fog collection work?

Fog is an inexpensive source of fresh water. But fog collection doesn't work everywhere. Scientists must consider many factors before deciding whether or not to build a fog collection system.

A SUITABLE PLACE Think about what you learned in Lesson 26. Some dry, arid places could benefit from fog collectors, but not all dry places can use them.

▶ *What would make one area ideal for fog collection and another area unsuitable?*

_____

_____

_____

_____

_____

WHERE WOULD YOU COLLECT FOG? Think of an area near your home or school where fog collection might work. Describe the area and what makes it a good place to collect fog. If there is no good place near you, imagine a perfect fog collection spot and describe it.

_____

_____

_____

_____

_____

UNIT 3: WATER ON EARTH

▶ Read

NOTEZONE

List the things that are necessary for fog collection to work.

Professor Pilar Cereceda was asked if other places in the world can benefit from fog collection. Here's her answer.

Where Can Fog Collection Work?

The most important requirement, obviously, is that there be a mountain near the coast and clouds, with the appropriate characteristics, that can be intercepted by that mountain. If the cloud is at the right altitude and the prevailing winds...[are favorable], then a layer of fog will skim the ground.

"Imagine, for thousands of years, the [people living in] deserts have watched clouds pass overhead, while practically dying of thirst. What we have achieved...is a successful system for taking droplets captured by the mesh and channeling them together where they become the miracle of...[drinkable] water that flows forth from a tap in each home. Although many places appear to meet the necessary requirements, it is always essential to carry out a professional evaluation in each case to determine the most suitable terrain."

To this end, Cereceda investigates clouds, the wind, and water flows on site with her rain gauges, anemometers, and fog collectors. "What we did in Chungungo is something we certainly want to try and adapt in other areas...."

---

appropriate: suitable, useful
intercepted: blocked
altitude: height above Earth's surface
prevailing winds: winds that usually blow from only one direction

essential: necessary
evaluation: a careful examination
terrain: features of the land
rain gauge: an instrument that measures the amount of rainfall
anemometer: an instrument that measures wind speed

From: de Luigi, Maria. "Pilar Cereceda (Chile)." *In Person.* International Development Research Centre. (www.idrc.ca/library/document/102386/cereceda.html))

MAKING DECISIONS Imagine that you are looking for places that can benefit from fog collection. The flowchart below shows that the first step is to visit the site. If it looks promising, you set up a test fog collector. Then you use the result of the test to make a decision. There are three possible decisions. For each description below, choose the best decision. Use the flowchart to see your choices.

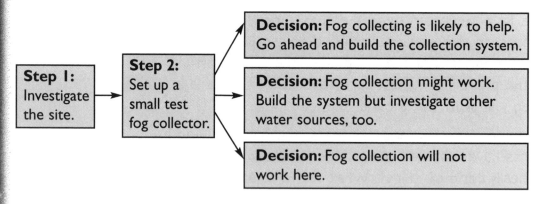

Step 1:
Investigate the site.

Step 2:
Set up a small test fog collector.

Decision: Fog collecting is likely to help. Go ahead and build the collection system.

Decision: Fog collection might work. Build the system but investigate other water sources, too.

Decision: Fog collection will not work here.

▶ *On your first site visit, you find a village on a foggy mountain. You visit again in the next season and find no fog for several months. Should you set up a test collector? Explain the reason for your decision.*

_____

_____

_____

▶ *You find that the fog collectors will have to be placed several kilometers away. Bringing water to the village will be expensive. What's your decision? Explain.*

_____

_____

_____

▶ *You find a village on a mountainside that gets fog all year long. The test collectors work. A nearby spring provides just enough fresh water for drinking and cooking. What's your decision? Explain.*

_____

_____

_____

CLEANING WATER

Build a model to find out how water is cleaned as it moves through the water cycle.

What You Need:

- large plastic bowl
- water
- dust and soil
- dark food coloring
- small, heavy drinking glass
- clear plastic wrap
- tape
- pebble

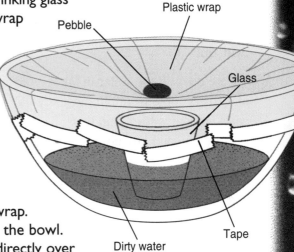

What to Do:

1. Pour water into the bowl until it is about 3 cm deep.
2. Mix dust and soil into the water. Add a few drops of food coloring.
3. Place the clean, dry glass right-side up in the center of the bowl.
4. Cover the bowl loosely with plastic wrap. Tape the edges of the plastic wrap to the bowl.
5. Place the pebble on the plastic wrap directly over the glass. The pebble should push the plastic down a bit. The plastic must not touch the glass.
6. Leave the bowl in full sunlight for a few hours.

WHAT DO YOU SEE? Look in the glass. Describe what you see.

_____

► Propose Explanations

HOW DOES IT WORK?

► *Explain what happened in your model.*

_____

_____

_____

_____

► *Explain why water that is collected from fog does not contain microorganisms.*

_____

_____

Bountiful River

COMING TOGETHER

One trickling stream doesn't hold much water. But water from a hundred trickling streams can add up.

Where does all the water in lakes and rivers come from? In most cases, it comes from rain that falls on the land around the lake or river. A *watershed* is an area of land that catches precipitation and channels it into a large body of water, such as a lake, river, or marsh. Since water runs from higher places to lower places, rain that falls on a mountain will run down the mountain until it reaches flat ground. Water that moves downhill across the land surface is known as *runoff*.

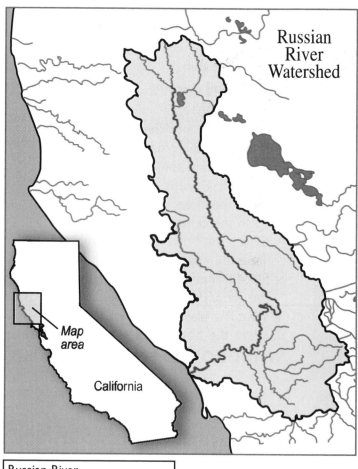

Russian River Watershed

Map area

California

Russian River ———
Tributaries ～～～
Watershed boundary ———

SCIENCE SAURUS

Divides and
 Drainage Basins 193
Water Pollution 352

SCI LINKS
THE WORLD'S A CLICK AWAY

www.scilinks.org
Keyword: Watersheds
Code: GSED13

▶ **Explore**

INTERPRETING A MAP The map above shows the watershed of the Russian River in northern California. The Russian River is shown in dark blue. All the streams and smaller rivers are shown in light blue. The streams and smaller rivers that feed into a larger river are known as *tributaries*.

▶ *Use a red pen or pencil to color the tributaries that feed into the Russian River.*

IDENTIFY YOUR WATERSHED

Get to know your own watershed.

What You Need:
- map of local area that shows streams, creeks, rivers, lakes, and ponds
- tracing paper
- masking tape
- clear tape
- blue, red, and black pencils

What to Do:
1. Find your school on the map.
2. Place the tracing paper over your school and the area of land around it. Hold the tracing paper in place with small pieces of masking tape at the corners.
3. Find the stream nearest to your school. Use a blue pencil to trace its entire length. Follow it upstream to its head (the place where it starts) and downstream until it reaches a river, lake, or marsh.
4. Use the blue pencil to trace all the smaller streams that also feed into that stream and into the river, lake, or marsh.
5. Use a red pencil to mark a dot at the head of each stream you traced. Then connect the dots.
6. Use the black pencil to label your school and the bodies of water on the map.
7. Add arrows to show the direction of water flow in the streams.
8. Add a legend to show the scale of your map. (Copy the legend from the map.)

What Do You See?
▶ *What does the red line connecting the dots show?*

_____

Think About It:
▶ *In what ways do people use the land in your watershed?*

_____

_____

▶ *What might pollute runoff as it flows over the land?*

_____

_____

▶ *How can pollutants dumped into small streams near your school or home affect a larger stream many miles away?*

_____

Bountiful River

Flooding a River

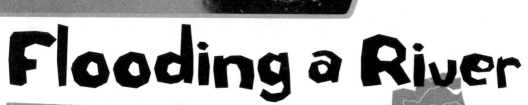

- Quabbin Reservoir

✳ Boston

MASSACHUSETTS

How do you turn a river into a lake?

In the early 1900s, the Swift River wandered through a valley in western Massachusetts. Along its banks were the towns of Enfield, Greenwich, Prescott, and Dana. People in these towns enjoyed their lives in the valley. But the valley that held these towns could also hold something else, and the water-hungry residents of the city of Boston knew it.

▶ Before You Read

THINK ABOUT IT When European settlers arrived in North America, they lived in small communities. Each community needed a water supply, so the settlers chose to live near a river, lake, or stream. As more settlers arrived, some small communities grew into large towns. As more people moved to the towns, some towns grew into cities. Soon the people in the cities did not have enough clean water to meet their needs.

▶ *What do you think a growing city could do to get enough clean water for its residents?*

_____

_____

_____

▶ Read

Here is how one growing city turned to its neighbors to get enough clean drinking water.

QUABBIN RESERVOIR

In the late 1800s, the Swift River Valley was an isolated but prosperous farming and industrial area as well as a vacation destination. The valley was a beautiful...spot.

In the 1890s, rumors began to circulate that Boston needed more water to slake the thirst of its ever-increasing population. As more and more people flowed into Boston, its existing water supply simply could not keep up with demand. More water would have to be found. The Swift River Valley fit all the criteria for a large reservoir. Boston would get the water it needed. But what would the cost be to the people of the Swift River Valley?

The cost would be the total annihilation of the valley. All homes, industries, and farms would have to be sold, moved, or destroyed. Everyone would have to leave. Even the graves would be dug up and the bodies reburied elsewhere. Thirty-nine square miles [101 km^2] of land would be cleared, burned, and flooded....

In 1927, the Massachusetts State Legislature officially declared [that] the valley would become the source of Boston's water supply, the Quabbin Reservoir. In 1933 and 1935, construction of [a dam] began. By 1939, the new reservoir began to fill, erasing four towns from the map.

isolated: set apart
prosperous: successful
slake: satisfy
criteria: requirements
reservoir: a human-made lake where water is stored for use by people
annihilation: destruction

From: "The Quabbin Reservoir," *The Connecticut River Homepage*. University of Massachusetts Department of Biology. (www.bio.umass.edu/biology/conn.river/quabbinres.html)

FIND OUT MORE

SCIENCESAURUS

Habitat Loss	341
Tradeoffs	369
Risk-Benefit Analysis	371

SCiLINKS
THE WORLD'S A CLICK AWAY

www.scilinks.org
Keyword: Rivers
Code: GSED14

BEFORE AND AFTER These photos of the Swift River Valley were all taken from the same location in different years. The first photo was taken in 1927 just after the decision was made to flood the valley. The second was taken in 1937 once preparations were complete and the valley was ready to flood. The third shows the reservoir filled with water years later in 1987.

1927

1937

1987

▶ *What things can you see in the 1927 photo that are absent in the 1937 photo?*

_____

▶ *On the 1937 photo, draw a curved line that separates the trees from the bare ground.*

Compare the line you drew and the water line in the 1987 photo.

▶ *How do you suppose engineers decided where to remove trees and where to leave them standing?*

_____

_____

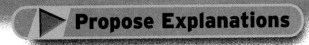

▶ Propose Explanations

GOOD AND BAD RESULTS Most decisions faced by communities have both costs and benefits. Costs are the bad—or negative—things that are results of the decision. Benefits are the good—or positive—things that are results of the decision.

▶ *According to the reading, what was the benefit of creating the Quabbin Reservoir? Who benefited?*

_____

_____

▶ *According to the reading, what were the costs? Who felt the costs the most?*

_____

_____

_____

The Quabbin watershed is protected from most human uses. Hunting, hiking, fishing, and some boating are allowed. Camping is not.

▶ *How does protecting the watershed protect the water in the reservoir?*

_____

_____

_____

▶ *How do you think creating the reservoir might have harmed wildlife?*

_____

_____

_____

▶ *How do you think creating the reservoir benefited wildlife?*

_____

_____

_____

▶ *What activities should not be allowed in or around a reservoir? Why?*

_____

_____

Bountiful River

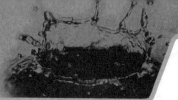

RESTORING A RIVER

Sometimes a river can be brought back to what it once was.

The need for water in any community is great. People use water for drinking, cooking, washing, and growing plants for food. Factories use large amounts of water. Farmers often get the water they need for crops by diverting it from nearby rivers. (Diverting a river means changing its direction of flow.) But this often harms wildlife that depends on the river. Groups that want river water for cities or farms and groups that want to protect rivers for wildlife argue about what to do.

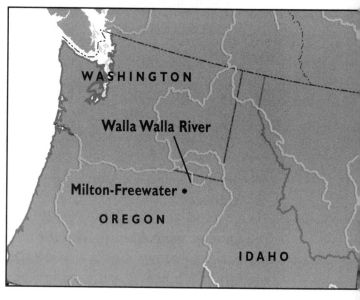

One river that groups argued over is the Walla Walla River in Washington state. The river is home to many fish and other wildlife. But over the past hundred years, much of the river's water has been diverted and used to water crops. An environmental group called WaterWatch was interested in restoring the river.

 **Before You Read**

GOODBYE TO WATER Think about a river you have seen—either a river in your area or one you have seen on TV. Now imagine that about half the water in the river will be diverted to supply farms and factories.

▶ *What changes in the river would you expect to see?*

_____

_____

_____

_____

▶ Read

Underline three main ideas in this reading.

A member of WaterWatch talks about the day he saw the Walla Walla River flowing again and what it took to get there.

Bringing Back the River

A few weeks ago I...witnessed something that has rarely...been seen [in] the past century: water flowing in the Walla Walla River on a hot August day.

What's so remarkable about water flowing in a river? In this case, plenty. Throughout the 20th century, the Walla Walla was completely dried up...at the town of Milton-Freewater every summer by irrigation diversions.... At the start of summer irrigation the river would dry up so abruptly that fish were left stranded in isolated pools. For 40 years, biologists would stun these fish with electric shockers, scoop them up in buckets and move them to wet parts of the river. [Then we discovered that] a few of those unlucky stranded fish were protected by the Endangered Species Act.

[Rather than fight each other in court,] WaterWatch and other conservation groups went to the Walla Walla [watershed] in April of 2000 to meet with the irrigators, and they made us feel welcome. We all shook hands, sat down at a table... and talked for several hours.

...The irrigators have committed to [return enough water to] permanently maintain flows in the river.... The river kept flowing all summer [this year], and... the fish didn't need to be rescued. This would be the first plan of its kind to restore river flows under the Endangered Species Act, and it won't be easy.

irrigation diversions: redirecting water from the natural path of the river to places where it can be used to water farm crops

abruptly: suddenly
isolated: set apart
permanently: all the time
maintain: keep

FIND OUT MORE

SCIENCESAURUS

Freshwater Ecosystems	148
Habitat Loss	341
Tradeoffs	369
Risk-Benefit Analysis	371

From: Benson, Reed. "Stream of Consciousness." *WaterWatch.* (www.waterwatch.org/instream.html#STREAM)

CONFLICTING INTERESTS

▶ *What two groups argued over the Walla Walla River?*

_____

_____

▶ *Describe each group's position on how Walla Walla River water should be used. What did each group want?*

_____

_____

_____

▶ *Why was it a problem that both groups wanted to use the river?*

_____

_____

_____

_____

A few species of wild fish managed to live in the river even with so little water. Two of these species were identified as being threatened with extinction. These fish were protected by law. The environmentalists could have taken the farmers to court for breaking the law protecting the fish. But they didn't.

▶ *How did the two groups find a compromise?*

_____

_____

_____

WHAT DO YOU THINK? Fish can be very choosy about where they lay their eggs. Many travel the length of a river to find the right spot.

▶ *How might diverting river water affect fish's ability to reproduce? How would the total number of fish be affected over time?*

_____

_____

_____

_____

▶ *How might leaving water in the river affect farmers? How would it affect consumers?*

_____

_____

_____

▶ **Take Action**

DO RESEARCH Is there a water battle going on in your area? Do some research to find out. Which body of water is in question? What is the issue about that water—water use, water quality, or another concern? Which groups are fighting about the water? What is each group's position?

In the space below, take notes about the issue in your area. List questions you'd like to ask local water specialists, wildlife experts, farmers, politicians, town planners, and business owners.

NOTES

_____

_____

_____

_____

_____

_____

QUESTIONS

_____

_____

_____

_____

_____

_____

Water Watch

FRESHWATER WORRIES

Clean clear water. We all need it—but for some, it's not easy to get.

Most of Earth's water (97%) is salt water, which people cannot drink. Only a tiny percentage is fresh water. Most of that is locked up in ice at the North and South poles and in glaciers. The little fresh liquid water that remains is not always available where and when people need it. An area may have no rain for months or even years. Then suddenly the area may be drenched by heavy downpours that cause floods.

Water pollution is also a concern around the world. Waste water from factories can pollute rivers, streams, lakes, and groundwater. (Groundwater is water in the ground that supplies wells.) Human and animal wastes can also pollute sources of fresh water.

 **Before You Read**

THINK ABOUT YOUR WATER Does your community ever experience water shortages? Try to imagine what it would be like not to have enough clean, fresh water to meet your needs. Think about all the ways that you and your family use water.

▶ *Which water uses should you stop during a water shortage? Which water uses are too important to stop?*

_____

_____

_____

_____

_____

_____

▶ **Read**

Too Little, Too Much

Hajara lives in Niger, West Africa, where the rainy season doesn't always bring enough fresh water to last the whole year.

It was one of the worst years my parents could remember. Each day, I had to walk 20 kilometers to find a well to fill my bucket. The walk back was the worst—the bucket was so heavy on my head that I swear my neck had shrunk by the time I got home.

One day, the well dried up and I had to look for water in the ponds. My mum had to boil it to get rid of the...microbes. This takes ages and you have to wait until it cools down before you can use it. But it's OK. It's what you have to do if you live in a dry, hot country.

Hajara Kader, Niger

Africa ▲

NOTEZONE

<u>Underline</u> the water sources Hajara uses.

Julie lives in the east African country of Kenya. Although Kenya is often dry, in 1997–1998 it had too much rain.

The rains started in October 1997 and ended in mid-April, 1998: six months of disaster in Kenya. People and animals drowned, crops were flooded, and bridges and roads were spoiled by the deluge of water. Even today, many of the roads have not been repaired in the poorer areas of the country. Waterborne diseases such as cholera, dysentery, typhoid and bilharzia increased due to the rains. In a developing country such as Kenya, people have a hard time finding the money to rebuild their homes. Where crops and farms were destroyed, others also lost their jobs.

Julie Nailantei, Kenya

NOTEZONE

If you could talk to Julie, what would you ask her?

FIND OUT MORE

SCIENCE SAURUS

Water Pollution 352
Surface and
Groundwater
Pollution 353

SCiLINKS
THE WORLD'S A CLICK AWAY

www.scilinks.org
Keyword: Water
Conservation
Code: GSED15

microbes: organisms too small to be seen without a microscope; some cause disease

deluge: a heavy downpour
waterborne: carried by water

From: "Fresh Water." *Pachamama*. United Nations Environment Programme. (www.unep.org/geo2000/pacha/fresh/fresh2.htm)

COMPARING DROUGHTS AND FLOODS Hajara's family suffered when their area had a drought, a long period of very dry conditions. Julie and her family suffered from floods.

▶ **What clues in each reading tell you that farming was difficult because of too little or too much water?**

_____

_____

▶ **How can having too little or too much water both contribute to the spread of disease?**

_____

_____

_____

_____

INTERPRETING GRAPHS The two circle graphs show how much of Earth's water can be used by people. Use the information in the graphs to answer the questions.

▶ *According to the first graph, what percentage of all water on Earth is usable by humans?*

_____

▶ *What makes 99.7 percent of Earth's water unusable by humans? (Hint: Think about what you read at the beginning of this lesson.)*

_____

_____

_____

_____

▶ *According to the second graph, where is most of the usable water?*

_____

_____

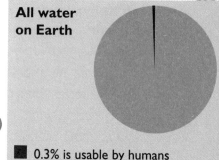

All water on Earth

■ 0.3% is usable by humans
□ 99.7% is unusable by humans

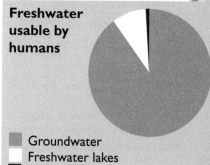

Freshwater usable by humans

■ Groundwater
□ Freshwater lakes
■ Rivers

USING PRECIOUS WATER People need water to drink. They also need it to irrigate crops and to use in manufacturing. The adjacent circle graph shows how fresh water is used around the world. Use the information in the graph to answer the questions below.

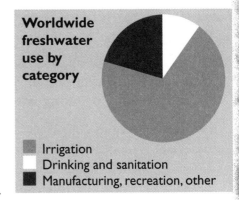

Worldwide freshwater use by category

- ▨ Irrigation
- ☐ Drinking and sanitation
- ■ Manufacturing, recreation, other

▶ *What is the largest use of fresh water? The smallest?*

_____

_____

▶ *The world's human population is growing. Scientists are looking for ways to conserve water—that is, reduce the water used for certain needs. Which category of use do you think they should try to conserve first? Explain your answer.*

_____

_____

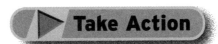

▶ Take Action

IMPROVE A TECHNOLOGY Some irrigation systems are simple canals dug next to crops. Water is pumped into the canals. As the water flows down the canals, nearby plants take in the water. The water in the canals is exposed to the hot sun. As water is heated, much of it evaporates and thus does not reach the plants.

▶ *How could this canal irrigation system be improved so that less fresh water is lost through evaporation? Draw, label, and write your ideas.*

Water Watch

HOLD THE SALT

You might sprinkle salt on your food. But you wouldn't want it in your drinking water!

Over 70 percent of our planet is covered by oceans. Unfortunately, the water is too salty for drinking, irrigation, and manufacturing. Long ago, people figured out that if they could remove the salts from ocean water, they'd have plenty of usable water. *Desalination* is the removal of salts and other substances from ocean water. It's a great idea—but it's not cheap.

▶ **Read**

There's more than one way to get the salts out of ocean water.

Fresh Water from Salt Water

People have been pulling fresh water out of the oceans for centuries using technologies that involve evaporation, which leaves the salts and other unwanted [substances] behind. Salty source water is heated to speed evaporation, and the evaporated water is then trapped and distilled. This process works well but requires large quantities of heat energy, and costs have been [too high] for nearly all but the wealthiest nations.... To make the process more affordable, modern distillation plants recycle heat from the evaporation step.

A potentially cheaper technology called membrane desalination may expand the role of desalination worldwide.... [In] membrane desalination,...a thin, semipermeable membrane [is placed] between a volume of saltwater and a volume of fresh water. The water on the salty side is highly pressurized to drive water molecules, but not salt and other [substances], to the pure side.... This process pushes fresh water out of salt water.

FIND OUT MORE

SCIENCESAURUS
Ocean Water   202

Although...[membrane desalination] plants can offer energy savings, the earliest membranes...were fragile,...had short life spans, [and were damaged by] contaminants in the source water.... Pretreatment [steps], such as filtering out sediments and bacteria, must be extremely rigorous.... A new generation of so-called thin composite membranes...are sturdier, provide better filtration, and may last up to 10 years.

distilled: purified a liquid by boiling it and then letting it condense

membrane: an extremely thin sheet of material

semipermeable: lets some materials through but not others

pressurized: placed under pressure

contaminants: substances that make another substance unclean

sediments: tiny particles that settle out of water

bacteria: one-celled organisms that do not have a nucleus; some cause disease

rigorous: strict

composite: made of more than one material

From: Martindale, Diane, and Peter Gleick. "Seeking New Sources: Sweating the Small Stuff." *Scientific American.*

▶ **Explore**

ANALYZE PROS AND CONS Identify the advantages and disadvantages of the two desalination methods described in the reading. Record your ideas in the chart.

DISTILLATION		MEMBRANE DESALINATION	
Advantages	**Disadvantages**	**Advantages**	**Disadvantages**

BUILD A DESALINATION DEVICE

Evaporative distillation is one way to get fresh water from salt water. But burning fuels to heat the water costs money. Sunlight is a cheaper source of heat. See how sunlight can be used to purify water.

What You Need:

- two 2-L plastic soda bottles, one painted black
- 30 cm clear plastic tubing, 1–2 cm in diameter
- duct tape
- 120 cm^3 table salt
- 1 L water
- large bowl
- small bowl
- spoon
- funnel
- block of wood

What to Do:

1. In the large bowl, mix the salt in 1 liter of water. Stir with a spoon until the salt is dissolved.
2. Pour about 5 mL of the salty water into the small bowl. Leave it overnight.
3. Put the funnel in the mouth of the black bottle. Pour in the remaining salt water. Rinse and dry the large bowl.
4. Put one end of the tubing in the black bottle. Use duct tape to seal the opening. Put the other end of the tubing in the clear bottle. The setup should look like the diagram on this page.
5. Put both bottles near a window where sunlight will hit them. Place the block under the black bottle. Leave both bottles alone for several days.

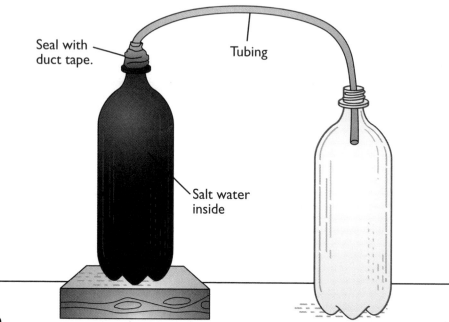

Seal with duct tape.

Tubing

Salt water inside

What Do You See?

▶ *What do you notice after several days?*

_____

_____

_____

Examine the small bowl.

▶ *What was left in it after the water evaporated?*

_____

Pour the water from the clear bottle into a bowl. Leave the water in the bowl to evaporate overnight.

▶ *What is left in the bowl? What can you infer about the water?*

_____

_____

_____

▶ *What do you think happened to the salt you dissolved in the water for the black bottle?*

_____

_____

_____

In Lesson 31, you read about water worries in Niger and Kenya. Look at the map on page 115 to see where each country is located.

▶ *Could this desalination method be useful in Niger? In Kenya? Explain.*

_____

_____

_____

_____

_____

Water Watch

ONE COOL IDEA

How do you move the world's biggest ice cube?

Antarctica, the continent around the South Pole, holds about 70 percent of the world's fresh water. The water is trapped in the form of a thick sheet of ice that covers the continent. Every so often, a large chunk of this ice breaks off and floats on the ocean's surface as an iceberg. The sight of a giant chunk of fresh water was too tempting for Professor Patrick Quilty. He had to figure out a way to get it to where it was needed most.

▶ **Read**

Look out, icebergs! Patrick Quilty is a man with a plan.

ICEBERGS TO AFRICA

Australian polar scientist Professor Patrick Quilty thinks he has a pretty cool idea. He wants to move Antarctic icebergs around the world for use as a source of [fresh] water.

Yes, icebergs.

Professor Quilty reckons it can be done by wrapping icebergs in huge, and he means HUGE, plastic bags and towing them to places like Africa where water is... scarce.

...[Professor Quilty] says if an iceberg [were] towed behind a ship, it would [melt] as it reached warmer waters. But...if it [were] wrapped in plastic, that could be avoided. The professor says a [fiber]-reinforced plastic is available that would hold the iceberg and the water as it [melts]. "You could actually get [the iceberg]...up to north-eastern Africa where there are drought areas, and then potentially provide a base for their food source...," he says.

polar: having to do with the North or South Pole
reckons: believes

scarce: in short supply
potentially: possibly

From: Fry, Sandra. "Icebergs to Africa." *Australian Broadcast Corporation.* (www.abc.net.au/news/features/antarctica/)

▷ Propose Explanations

RIVERS OF WATER Professor Quilty has an idea about how nature can help move the icebergs. Look at the map below. It shows the pattern of currents—rivers of water—that move through Earth's oceans. These currents carry floating objects along with them. "Aha!" thinks Professor Quilty.

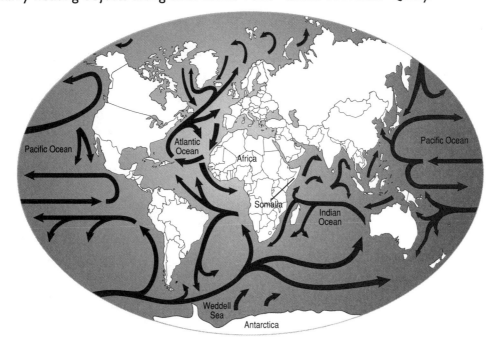

▶ *Look at the ocean currents that flow between Antarctica and Africa. Explain how a combination of drifting and towing could be used to move an iceberg from Antarctica to drought-stricken Somalia in northeast Africa.*

_____

_____

_____

_____

_____

_____

▶ *To what other places could an iceberg be moved using ocean currents and towing?*

_____

_____

Current Events

OCEAN RIVERS

It's strange, but true—rivers run through oceans. And some surprising things are floating around.

Each year, ships carry more than 100 million containers across Earth's oceans. The containers are the size of large trucks and sit on the ships' open decks. Many are filled with products that are made in one place and sold in another. Doll heads, bath toys, and sneakers are some of the items that make the long voyage across the ocean. Sometimes a cargo ship runs into stormy weather. Then containers can fall off a ship and be lost at sea. But that doesn't stop some of this cargo from reaching shore!

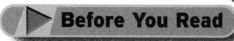

▶ **Before You Read**

OCEAN IN MOTION Did you ever see a movie about a storm at sea? Watch the waves at the shore? Go deep-sea fishing? Seen people surfing, live or on TV?

▶ *List all the kinds of motion you can think of that take place in the ocean.*

_____

_____

_____

_____

_____

_____

_____

_____

▶ Read

NOTEZONE

What carried the sneakers to shore?

What kinds of lost cargo might make it to shore?

What kinds might not make it?

What happens when 60,000 sneakers fall into the ocean? Here's the story of their wet journey from Asia to North America.

These Shoes Just Did It

Surface currents in the oceans move in large slow circles called gyres. That explains the story of 60,000 Nike shoes [that] spilled from a storm-tossed cargo ship in the northeastern Pacific in May 1990.

Six months to a year later, beachcombers from British Columbia to Oregon began to find shoes. Oceanographers constructed a computer model that predicted the shoes' route. In 1993, shoes were found in Hawaii….

The shoes...were wearable after a scrubbing to remove barnacles, algae, and tar.

---

surface current: a river of water pushed along the ocean's surface by winds

beachcomber: a person who looks for objects that have washed ashore on a beach

oceanographer: a scientist who studies the ocean

barnacle: a hard-shelled ocean animal that attaches itself to surfaces

algae: plant-like organisms that live in water and carry out photosynthesis

From: "Staying On Top: These Shoes Just Did It." *Ocean Planet.* Smithsonian Institution. (seawifs.gsfc.nasa.gov/OCEAN_PLANET/HTML/oceanography_currents_2.html)

FIND OUT MORE

SCIENCESAURUS

Ocean Currents	203
Surface Ocean Currents	204
Coriolis Effect	205

SCI LINKS
THE WORLD'S A CLICK AWAY

www.scilinks.org
Keyword: Ocean Currents
Code: GSED16

INTERPRETING A MAP The map below shows the movement of the North Pacific gyre, a system of surface currents in the Pacific Ocean. The numbers show where Nike sneakers from the lost container were found on different dates in the early 1990s.

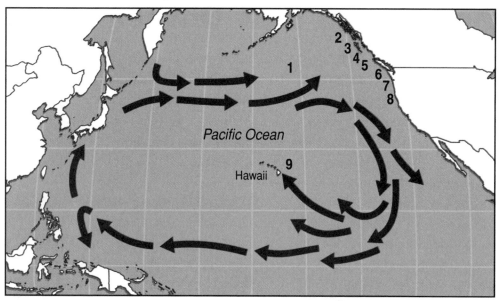

❶ shoe spill	May 27, 1990	❻ 150 recovered	April 4, 1991
❷ 200 recovered	Nov.–Dec. 1990	❼ 200 recovered	May 9–10, 1991
❸ 100 recovered	Jan.–Feb. 1991	❽ 200 recovered	May 18, 1991
❹ 200 recovered	Feb.–March 1991	❾ several recovered	Jan.–March 1993
❺ 250 recovered	March 26, 1991		

MAKE INFERENCES Where do you think the sneakers landed next? (If you need to, refer to a world map or globe.) Explain.

_____

_____

_____

▶ *The map shows that about 1,300 sneakers were found. What do you think happened to the almost 59,000 other sneakers lost at sea?*

_____

_____

_____

_____

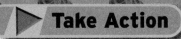

GENERATE QUESTIONS The paths of ocean currents change direction slightly from season to season and from year to year. Whatever sneakers are still out there may be found in the future.

Imagine you are an oceanographer who is using the sneakers to study ocean currents in the northern Pacific. Design a poster to put up at beaches. On it, ask people to look out for sneakers. Tell them why the sneakers are there. (Make sure they know they can keep the sneakers!) Include some questions that will give scientists studying ocean currents more information to add to the map. Ask people to send answers to the questions. Write your message and questions below.

_____

_____

_____

_____

_____

_____

_____

_____

_____

_____

_____

_____

_____

_____

_____

_____

_____

_____

_____

Current Events

BEACHCOMBER SCIENTIST

Can a sneaker be a tool of scientific research? Ask an oceanographer!

Quick! Think of all the things you can do with a sneaker. Chances are that doing scientific research didn't come to mind. It wasn't on oceanographer Curtis Ebbesmeyer's mind either. But sometimes doing scientific research is simply a matter of observing something that's already out there— like hundreds of sneakers that wash up on beaches all around the Pacific Ocean.

▶ Before You Read

EVERYDAY SCIENCE Not all science is done in a laboratory. And scientific discoveries don't always require fancy equipment. Sometimes things that happen right around you can lead to new discoveries. You just need to keep an open mind to new ideas.

▶ *Write about a time when you made an interesting discovery about the natural world. What were you doing? What did you notice? What new ideas did you have?*

_____

_____

_____

_____

_____

_____

_____

_____

▶ Read

NOTEZONE

(Circle) all the items that Ebbesmeyer used to track ocean currents.

New scientific ideas often come from unexpected places. Meet a beachcomber scientist who still learns from his mom.

Tracking Currents With Sneakers

Every year, more than 10,000 containers fall overboard and spill their cargo into the ocean. Storms are often to blame. An 8-foot by 40-foot [2.43-meter by 12.1-meter] container, which can carry up to 58,000 pounds [26,308.4 kilograms] of cargo, might hold 10,000 shoes, 17,000 hockey gloves, or a million Legos.

[Oceanographer Curtis] Ebbesmeyer and his partners... design and manufacture instruments that measure ocean currents.... Until 1990, Ebbesmeyer dropped buoys, drift cards, and markers into the sea to track current flows without giving much thought to what was already adrift. But when his mom quizzed him about where beach junk comes from, he realized that the ocean was filled with readymade markers whose course he could plot from ship to shore.

buoy: a marker, often with a bell or light, designed to float on the ocean's surface

drift cards: floating cards used to track the paths of currents

plot: locate on a map

From: Podsada, Janice. "Beach: Nike Shoes Wash Up." *The Daily Herald* (Everett, WA)

▶ Propose Explanations

THINKING LIKE A SCIENTIST Ebbesmeyer listened to his mom's question and thought about it carefully, even though she is not an oceanographer. How is this an example of good scientific habits?

_____

_____

_____

_____

_____

FIND OUT MORE

SCIENCESAURUS

Surface Ocean Currents   204

Current Events

Electricity From the Sea

How can we get useful electrical energy from ocean currents? Some scientists are coming up with ideas!

Windmills can change the energy of steady winds into electrical energy. Can the steady force of water currents do the same thing? A group of scientists and engineers in Norway think so. Currents move through the ocean in many parts of the world. In some places, the water is shallow enough so that a "wind mill" can be placed on the seabed to reach the current. So if it works in Norway, it might work in other places, too.

► **Before You Read**

ENERGY RESOURCES There are lots of ways to produce electrical energy. Some are listed in the following chart. What other ways can you think of? Add them to the chart. Then list the advantages and disadvantages of each one. Maybe you'll have an idea that no one has thought of yet!

Ways to Produce Electrical Energy	Advantages	Disadvantages
From wind	Wind is free and cannot run out.	Many places don't get steady winds.
From burning coal		
From burning oil and natural gas		

▶ Read

NOTEZONE

Underline the descriptions of ocean currents in the sound.

Which current could destroy a water mill?

The team from Norway has a plan. They are trying to use the force of ocean currents to generate electricity. Here's their idea.

"Water Mills"
at the Bottom of the Sea

Because water is 850 times as dense as air, ocean currents are much more powerful than the wind. This source of power is about to be [used] in a novel way in Hammerfest, [Norway], where the Hammerfest Power Company plans to build 20 water mills on the seabed. The mills are based on the same principle as wind turbines, and they will be placed in the sound between the island of Kvaloy and the mainland. Current speeds in the sound can be as high as 2.5 meters per second, and each turbine will generate 300–800 [kilowatts] of electricity....

Scientists will measure the strength of the eddy currents in the sound.... Eddies are capable of destroying a turbine by [forcing] unequal loads on its blades. The next stage will be to develop the turbine rotor. Again, because of the great power of water currents, the rotors of a water turbine must be able to withstand much greater loads than wind turbines.... The test model, which is currently being developed, will be tested before a prototype is built.

---

dense: having particles that are packed close together

novel: new

turbine: a machine that uses paddles or blades to convert the energy of moving air or water into another form of energy

sound: a body of water between an island and the mainland

eddy: a smaller current that runs in a different direction from the main current

load: weight or stress

rotor: the rotating blades of a turbine

prototype: an early model or design

From: Gisvold, Magne. "'Water Mills' at the Bottom of the Sea." *SINTEF Publications*. SINTEF Energy Research. (www.sintef.no/publications/pro_eng_24.html)

FIND OUT MORE

SCIENCESAURUS

Ocean Currents 203
Subsurface
  Currents 206
Renewable Energy
  Resources 328

▶ Propose Explanations

ANALYZE ADVANTAGES A team of American scientists is designing its own water mill to convert the energy of an ocean current into electrical energy. The Gulf Stream is a surface current in the western Atlantic Ocean. It carries water north along the eastern coast of the United States. At its fastest, the Gulf Stream current moves at more than 2 meters (6.5 feet) per second.

Although it officially starts off the coast of North Carolina, the Gulf Stream is fed by water from the Florida Current. On the map you can see the start of the Florida Current between the southern tip of Florida and Cuba. The arrows show the direction and speed of the current. The longer the arrow, the faster the current moves. The closer a current is to shore, the shallower the water.

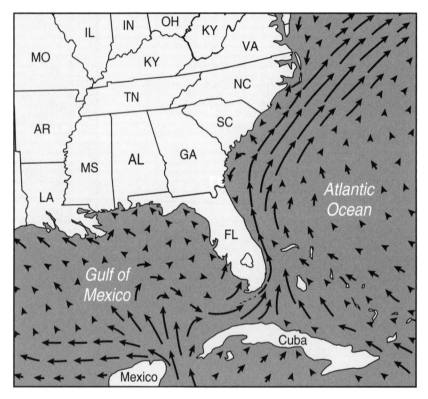

▶ *The American team chose to test its water mill off the southeast coast of Florida. Why do you think they chose that location?*

_____

_____

_____

_____

_____

_____

▶ Once the *Gulf Stream* moves past North Carolina, how does it change direction? What would this mean for scientists looking for places to put their water mills?

_____

_____

_____

_____

▶ **Take Action**

GIVE A NEWS REPORT You are a television science reporter. Your boss gives you two minutes of airtime to report on the water mill plan for the Gulf Stream. Write a script of what you will say. First, write an outline of your script below. Decide what pictures you will need. Remember to include Who, What, When, Where, Why, and How. Make your report interesting and accurate. When you have written your draft, have someone time you as you read it. Make sure your report is two minutes long.

_____

_____

_____

_____

_____

_____

_____

_____

_____

_____

_____

Weather and Climate

How does weather affect our lives?

We consult a weather report to prepare ourselves for the day ahead—to find out if we'll need an umbrella or sunscreen or snow boots. What happens in the air above us to cause different kinds of weather? And how do people handle severe weather conditions, such as a hurricane or blizzard?

In this unit you'll explore weather and climate. Air pressure—the weight of the air pushing down on you—plays a major role in determining the weather. You'll learn how differences in air pressure produced one of the most violent storms ever to hit the Northeast and how weather forecasters tried to protect fishing boats out at sea. You'll read about other kinds of severe weather—tornadoes, hailstorms, and blizzards. You'll find out how trees can tell scientists what the climate was like thousands of years ago. Then you'll travel to the Arctic to study ice conditions that may tell scientists whether our global climate is changing.

? Did You Know?
How fast a tree cricket chirps is affected
by temperature. Listen to a cricket chirp.
Count how many chirps it makes in 15
seconds, then add 37 to that number.
Your result will be close to the actual
air temperature in degrees Fahrenheit.

The Atmosphere

Feeling the Pressure?

On some days, the air presses on you with greater force, on other days with lesser force.

You may think air is just empty space, but it's actually made of molecules that have weight. Because air has weight, it pushes down on everything it touches—including people! The more air there is above you, the more it pushes down on you. As a result, air pressure is lower the higher you go in the atmosphere. At higher altitudes, air molecules are spread farther apart.

Air pressure is measured with an instrument called a barometer. The first barometer was built by Italian scientist Evangelista Torricelli in 1643. He filled a bowl with mercury, a metal that is liquid at room temperature. Then he also used mercury to fill a thin glass tube that was closed at one end. He turned the tube upside down with the open end in the bowl of mercury. The mercury did not run out—it stayed at a certain height in the tube. Above the mercury, at the top of the tube, was a vacuum—a space with no air in it. When the air pressure outside the tube increased, it pushed down more on the mercury in the bowl. As a result, the mercury went up higher in the tube. When the outside air pressure decreased, it pushed down less on the mercury in the bowl, and the mercury in the tube dropped down lower in the tube. (Caution: Do not try to repeat Torricelli's experiment! Mercury is poisonous.)

Torricelli barometer ▶

Explore

GET AIR Air pressure changes from day to day in the same place. These changes are measured and used in weather forecasts. Look at the two diagrams of Torricelli barometers below.

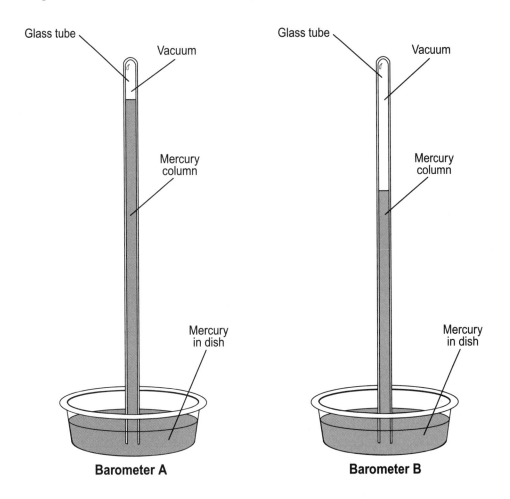

Barometer A

Barometer B

▶ *Which barometer shows higher air pressure?*

_____

▶ *Which barometer shows lower air pressure?*

_____

▶ *Draw arrows on both diagrams to show how strongly the air is pushing down on the mercury. Use thick arrows for higher air pressure and thin arrows for lower air pressure.*

FIND OUT MORE

SCIENCESAURUS

Earth's
Atmosphere 213
Air Pressure 224

www.scilinks.org
Keyword: Atmospheric
Pressure and Winds
Code: GSED17

The Atmosphere

UP, UP, AND AWAY

Ride a balloon into the skies with two explorers.

In 1783, people began trying to fly by filling balloons with hot, light air. The first balloons rose only about 100 meters, but scientists kept trying. Later balloons were filled with hydrogen and other "lighter-than-air" gases. Scientists wanted to know what was above the layer of air we live in, now called the troposphere. In 1862, scientist James Glaisher and pilot Henry Coxwell had the courage to explore this high frontier.

▶ Before You Read

THE AIR UP THERE You've probably read reports or seen TV shows about people who climb Mount Everest, the highest mountain in the world at 29,028 feet (8,845 meters, 8.845 kilometers).

▶ *What problem does high altitude create for mountain climbers? What do you think causes this problem?*

_____

_____

_____

▶ Read

In 1862, Henry Coxwell and James Glaisher flew a balloon 1.5 miles (2.5 kilometers) higher than the summit of Mount Everest.

HiGH FLYERS

As Glaisher patiently recorded what his instruments told him, the four mile [6.4 km] and five mile [8 km] marks were passed. Both men knew they were in line for a record. As Coxwell climbed into the rigging to free the valve line, Glaisher's eyesight began to deteriorate. He began to lose the power to move his arms and legs. His voice goes, his hearing fades. He passes out....

UNIT 4: WEATHER AND CLIMATE

Coxwell, in the rigging, is frozen almost helpless with the cold. His hands are turning blue and black. He tumbles, rather than climbs down into the basket. The balloon is still rising. Coxwell seizes the gas valve rope in his teeth and pulls. The valve opens and the balloon begins to descend.

Neither man appreciates the situation until afterwards when the instruments are read. But they have reached the 37,000 feet [11,300 m] mark. They are the first men in the stratosphere.

Without oxygen, without pressure suits, without a protective cabin, seven miles [11.3 km] high, they have penetrated into Jumbo Jet country.

Underline the words that tell how one of the explorers suffered from a lack of oxygen.

rigging: the ropes that tie the balloon to its basket

valve line: the tube that opens the balloon to release hot air

deteriorate: become worse

basket: the open compartment at the base of the balloon that carries the balloonists

seizes: grabs

descend: move downward

stratosphere: the layer of the atmosphere above the troposphere

pressure suits: special clothing worn to provide oxygen at a safe air pressure

penetrated: entered

From: Marion, Fulgence. *Wonderful Balloon Ascents: or the Conquest of the Skies.*

FIND OUT MORE

SCIENCESAURUS

Earth's
  Atmosphere   213
Composition of
  the Atmosphere 214
Layers of the
  Atmosphere   215
Kinds of Graphs   390
Line Graphs   394
Making a Line
  Graph   395–399

► Explore

READ A DATA TABLE This table shows the measurements you might make if you went up in a balloon. The abbreviation *hPa* stands for hectopascals, a unit used to measure air pressure.

▶ *Which altitude on the data table is closest to the highest point that Glaisher and Coxwell reached?*

▶ *What would the temperature have been at that altitude?* _____

▶ *Where on Earth's surface do you think you might find temperatures that low?*

Altitude	Air Temperature	Air Pressure
0 m	15°C	1,013 hPa
1,000 m	8.5°C	900 hPa
2,000 m	2°C	800 hPa
3,000 m	−4.5°C	700 hPa
4,000 m	−11°C	620 hPa
5,000 m	−17.5°C	540 hPa
6,000 m	−24.5°C	470 hPa
7,000 m	−30.5°C	410 hPa
8,000 m	−37°C	360 hPa
9,000 m	−43.5°C	310 hPa
10,000 m	−50°C	260 hPa
11,000 m	−56.5°C	230 hPa
12,000 m	−56.5°C	190 hPa

MAKE A GRAPH

Have you ever plotted two kinds of data on the same type of graph? Try it with air pressure and temperature. Use the two grids below to graph the data in the table on page 139.

What You Need:
- two colors of pencils

What to Do:

1. On both graphs, label the horizontal axis "Altitude (meters)."
2. On the horizontal axis, find the highest point that Coxwell and Glaisher reached. Write "highest point" below this altitude.
3. Label the left graph's vertical axis "Air Temperature (°C)."
4. Label the right graph's vertical axis "Air Pressure (hPa)."
5. While plotting one graph, place a strip of paper over the data for the other graph to avoid confusion.
6. Use one color pencil on the left graph. Plot a point for the temperature at each altitude listed in the table. Then draw a line to connect the points.
7. Use a second color pencil for the right graph. Plot a point for the air pressure at each altitude. Then draw a line to connect the points.
8. Add a title to each graph.

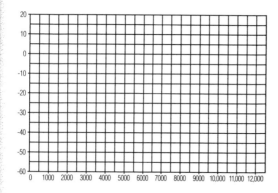
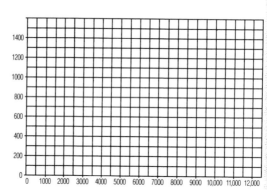

ANALYZE YOUR GRAPHS

► *How does air pressure change as you go higher into the atmosphere?*

_____

► *How does air temperature change as you go higher into the atmosphere?*

_____

MAKE INFERENCES During their balloon ride, Glaisher suffered from altitude sickness. Altitude sickness is caused by not enough oxygen in the air that a person is breathing.

▶ *Was it the change in air temperature or the change in air pressure that caused Glaisher's altitude sickness? Explain your answer. (Hint: Recall what you learned in the previous lesson about air molecules at higher altitudes.)*

_____

_____

_____

_____

_____

_____

_____

_____

 **Take Action**

REAL WORLD PROBLEMS Glaisher and Coxwell had many problems on their balloon ride. Imagine taking a high-altitude balloon ride today.

▶ *What problems would you want to avoid? What do you think you could do to prevent those problems? Fill in the graphic organizer below.*

Problems	Solutions

The Atmosphere

Thar She Blows!

Hot-air balloon rides, kite flying, sailing—all these activities depend on wind.

Heat from the sun warms Earth's surface. Heat from the surface radiates into the air above it, heating the atmosphere. As the atmosphere warms, the air becomes less dense. This less dense air rises. As a result, the place it rose from becomes an area of lower pressure. Cooler air—which is more dense—flows into the lower pressure area. Air moving from an area of higher pressure to an area of lower pressure produces wind. When the difference in air pressure between the two areas increases, the wind blows stronger from the higher to the lower pressure areas.

▶ Before You Read

EXAMINE A SATELLITE IMAGE This photograph taken from a satellite shows the California coast and Pacific Ocean. The wispy grey areas extending out from the coastline are clouds of airborne dust. The bright white areas at the bottom of the photograph are regular clouds of water droplets.

▶ *Where do you think the dust comes from? What moves the dust out over the ocean?*

_____

_____

_____

_____

_____

_____

_____

_____

Satellite image of southern California ▶

Winds are named for the direction they blow *from*. Draw an arrow on the photo on page 142 to show the direction that the Santa Ana winds blow.

▶ **Read**

Winds whip through the narrow canyons along the coast of southern California.

Riding the Wind

Any allergy-stricken southern Californian can tell you when the Santa Ana winds are blowing. Recently, Santa Anas blew through the southland at speeds [greater than] 80 kilometers (50 miles) per hour.

A new image from [a satellite camera] on NASA's *Terra* spacecraft shows the pattern of airborne dust stirred up by Santa Ana winds on February 9, 2002. These dry, northeasterly winds usually occur in late fall and winter when a high pressure system forms in the Great Basin between the Sierra Nevada and Rocky Mountain ranges. The strength of the winds enables them to pick up and relocate surface dust.

allergy: extreme sensitivity to certain substances
Santa Ana winds: local winds that blow from the northeast in southern California
southland: the area in the south of a region
high pressure system: a large mass of dense air

From:"Santa Ana Winds Swirl Over Southern California."
NASA Jet Propulsion Laboratory. California Institute of Technology.
(www.jpl.nasa.gov/releases/2002/release_2002_43.html)

FIND OUT MORE

SCIENCESAURUS
Air Pressure	224
Wind	225

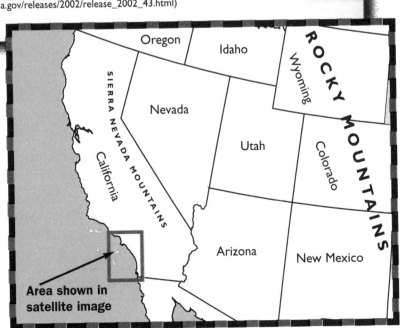

Area shown in satellite image

AIR PRESSURE AND THE SANTA ANAS The map below shows air pressure readings. Locations with the same air pressure are connected with lines called *isobars*. The isobars outline large air masses and show whether the air pressure in the masses is high or low.

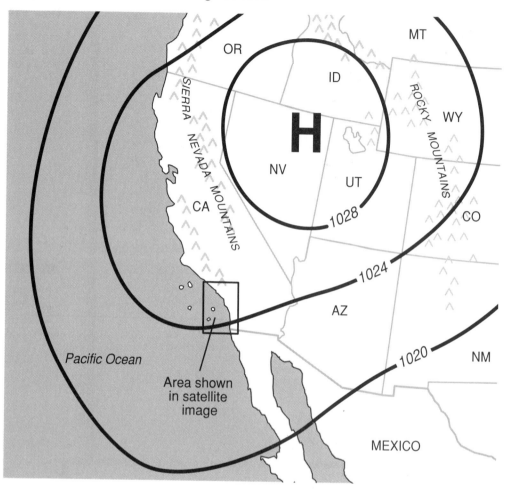

The Great Basin area of the United States lies between the Sierra Nevada Mountains and the Rocky Mountains. It includes all of Nevada and parts of the surrounding states.

▶ *Use a colored pencil to lightly shade the Great Basin.*

A high pressure system, like the one over the Great Basin on the map, is a large mass of dense air. The dense air sinks and moves outward from the center of the high in a clockwise direction. This flow of air causes wind.

▶ *Draw an arrow on each isobar line to show the direction in which the wind is moving in the Great Basin high pressure system.*

DUST IN THE WIND Look again at the satellite image on page 142. The darker areas are mountains covered with trees and other plants. Areas of the Great Basin east of the mountains look lighter because they have few or no trees and other plants.

▶ *Did the dust shown in the photograph come from the mountains or from the Great Basin? Explain your reasoning.*

_____

_____

_____

▶ *Santa Ana winds move through narrow canyons. As they do, they pick up speed. How would the Santa Ana winds affect any wildfires in that area?*

_____

_____

▶ Take Action

INVESTIGATE YOUR LOCAL WINDS The Santa Ana winds are called local winds because they occur in a small area. Sea breezes are another type of local wind. They occur in areas near the ocean. Mountain breezes and valley breezes are other examples of local winds.

Research local winds in your area. Find out what kind of wind it is (a sea breeze or valley breeze, for example) and when it blows—the time of day or season of the year. Find out what causes the wind. Draw and label a simple map of your area to show the direction and pattern of your local winds.

Stormy Weather

Predicting a Storm

Weather is more predictable if you have the right tools.

A meteorologist studies the atmosphere and weather and makes weather predictions. Once in a while, a prediction will surprise a meteorologist. Meteorologist Bob Case worked for the National Weather Service back in 1991, when "the perfect storm" hit. In fact, he came up with the phrase "the perfect storm." Case's job was to forecast the weather for the New England states and the ocean alongside them. Reports came from a powerful computer in Maryland. Case read the data and knew what was coming. In spite of the sunny weather along the coast, a big storm was forming out at sea.

At the same time, fishing boats, huge ocean cargo ships, and sailboats were out on the ocean. All used weather reports to plan their routes and stay out of a storm's way. They depended on Bob Case's forecasts to make those decisions.

▼ **An approaching storm off Newport, RI**

 **Before You Read**

WEATHER REPORT Meteorologists use many kinds of information to make their predictions. These predictions are used for weather forecasts on television, the radio, the Web, and in newspapers.

▶ *Think about the weather forecasts you have seen, read, or heard. List all the kinds of weather information presented. Describe the sorts of weather images that are used.*

_____

_____

_____

_____

_____

_____

▶ **Read**

NOTEZONE

Jot down a
question
about the
reading to ask
your teacher.

Here's how Bob Case got the information he needed to predict what he later named "the perfect storm."

Collecting Weather Data

October 28th is a sharp, sunny day in Boston, temperatures in the fifties with a stiff wind blowing off the ocean. A senior meteorologist named Bob Case is crisscrossing the carpeted room, consulting with the various meteorologists on duty that day. Most of them are seated at heavy blue consoles staring...at columns of numbers—barometric pressure, dew point, visibility—scrolling down computer screens....

A satellite photo of a hurricane about to clobber the coast of Maryland hangs in...[Case's] office. He is responsible for issuing regional forecasts based on satellite imagery and a nationwide system...[of weather] data-collection points....

Since early the previous day, Case has been watching something called a "short-wave trough aloft" slide eastward from the Great Lakes. On satellite photos it looks like an S-curve in the line of clear dry air moving south from Canada....The trough moves east at forty miles [64 km] an hour, strengthening as it goes. It follows the Canadian border to Montreal, cuts east across Northern Maine, crosses the Bay of Fundy, and traverses Nova Scotia throughout the early hours of October 28th. By dawn an all-out gale is raging north of Sable Island.

---

console: a monitor and keyboard that are connected to a computer system

barometric pressure: a measure of the pressure that air exerts in a certain place at a certain time

dew point: the temperature at which water vapor changes to liquid water

visibility: the clearness of the atmosphere

satellite imagery: pictures produced with data collected by satellites

trough: an elongated area of low barometric pressure

traverses: goes across

gale: a strong wind with speeds up to 87 km/h

From: Junger, Sebastian. *The Perfect Storm: A True Story of Men Against the Sea.* Harper Collins.

FIND OUT MORE

SCIENCESAURUS

Meteorology	212
Weather	218
Collecting Weather Data	219
Weather Maps and Symbols	220
Air Pressure	224
Wind	225

INTERPRETING SATELLITE IMAGERY

The satellite image at the right shows Hurricane Grace off the coast of the eastern United States.

Hurricane Grace

▶ *What does Hurricane Grace look like on this satellite image?*

_____

_____

▶ *Describe the location and size of Hurricane Grace. Use a U.S. map as a reference.*

_____

_____

_____

READING AIR PRESSURE MAPS

Barometric pressure is an important factor in predicting the weather. If barometric pressure is high or rising, there usually will be sunny skies and dry weather. If barometric pressure is low or falling, there usually will be clouds and stormy weather.

Study the map. Each line, called an *isobar*, connects places with the same barometric pressure. When the line makes a complete circle, the area inside the line is labeled either H or L. H stands for the center of a high-pressure area. L stands for the center of a low-pressure area.

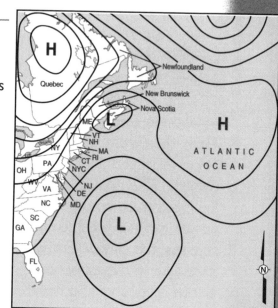

▶ *Where on the map do you see lows?*

_____

_____

▶ *Where on the map do you see highs?*

_____

Air flows from areas of higher pressure into areas of lower pressure. The closer the isobars are, the stronger the wind.

▶ *Where are the isobars very close together on this map?*

_____

148

▶ Propose Explanations

THINK IT OVER

▶ *How does having outlines of U.S. states and Canadian provinces make it easier for meteorologists to interpret the satellite images?*

_____

_____

Surface barometric pressure readings come into government weather offices several times a day. In the Atlantic Ocean there are floating buoys with instruments that measure and transmit pressure readings every two hours. Weather forecasters like Bob Case watch these readings looking for changes. From his Boston office, Case watched the barometric pressure drop over the ocean near Nova Scotia, Canada.

▶ *What kind of weather would a meteorologist have predicted for boats and ships in that area of the ocean? Explain.*

_____

_____

▶ Take Action

ANALYZE AIR PRESSURE DATA

Collect a barometric pressure reading at about the same time every day for one week. Also note the weather each day. You can obtain the measurements by using a barometer, listening to radio weather reports, or going online. Record the day, time, and reading in the table. Include units of barometric pressure as part of your reading.

Date & Time	Air Pressure (Units _____)	Weather Description

▶ *Did the barometric pressure rise, fall, or stay about the same from one day to the next?*

_____

▶ *If the barometric pressure stays about the same from day to day, what can you predict about the weather?*

_____

Stormy Weather

A STORM LIKE NO OTHER

A small fishing boat is no match for a violent storm.

The cold ocean waters off the coast of eastern Canada are home to thousands of swordfish during the warmer half of the year. Swordfishing boats go out for weeks at a time to catch this valuable fish. Unfortunately, these waters are located on one of the worst storm paths in the world. Weather there can change quickly. Storms can be powerful and dangerous—especially when three weather systems collide.

The swordfishing boat *Andrea Gail* sailed from Gloucester, Massachusetts, on September 20, 1991. It was last heard from at 6 P.M. on October 28, 1991. At that time, the boat was in the low-pressure area near Sable Island and Nova Scotia. This Sable Island storm was one of the three weather systems that helped form "the perfect storm."

▶ Before You Read

SEVERE WEATHER Depending on where you live, the word *storm* may bring different pictures to mind. Hurricanes, hailstorms, thunderstorms, blizzards, and tornadoes are common in some places and rare in others.

▶ *Write about one kind of storm you know well. Describe the weather conditions before, during, and after the storm.*

_____

_____

_____

_____

_____

_____

_____

_____

UNIT 4: WEATHER AND CLIMATE

▶ Read

While the *Andrea Gail* fights to stay afloat in huge waves, things get worse for all ships in the area.

HURRICANE GRACE

Hurricane Grace...has been quietly slipping up the [U.S.] coast. At 8 A.M. on the 29th, Grace collides with the cold front, as predicted, and goes reeling back out to sea. She's moving extremely fast and packing eighty-knot [148 km/hr] winds and thirty-foot [nine-meter] seas.... Grace crosses the 40th parallel that afternoon. At 8 P.M. on October 29th, Hurricane Grace runs into the Sable Island storm.

The effect is instantaneous....The wind starts rushing into the low at speeds up to a hundred miles [160 km] an hour. As a NOAA disaster report put it...a year later, "The dangerous storm previously forecast was now fact...."

The bulk carrier *Zarah*, just fifty miles [81 km] south of the *Andrea Gail* takes ninety-foot [27-meter] seas over her decks that shear off the steel bolts holding her portholes down. Thirty tons of water flood the...crew's sleeping quarters...and kill the ship's engine. The *Zarah* is 550 feet [168 meters] long.

The *Andrea Gail* was 70 feet (22 meters) long. Sketch how big it would look next to the *Zarah*.

cold front: the leading edge of a mass of cold air; cold fronts can bring violent storms

reeling: spinning

knot: a measurement of speed at sea or in the air; one nautical mile (1.852 km) per hour

parallel: also called line of latitude; an imaginary line that shows distance north or south of the equator

NOAA: National Oceanic and Atmospheric Administration (the National Weather Service)

bulk carrier: a large ship used to carry loose cargo such as coal or grain

shear: cut

porthole: a window in the side of a ship

From: Junger, Sebastian. *The Perfect Storm: A True Story of Men Against the Sea.* Harper Collins.

FIND OUT MORE

SCIENCESAURUS

Weather	218
Collecting Weather Data	219
Weather Maps and Symbols	220
Air Masses	221
Weather Fronts	222
Air Pressure	224
Wind	225

SCI LINKS
THE WORLD'S A CLICK AWAY

www.scilinks.org
Keyword: Storms
Code: GSED18

The Fisherman's Memorial at Gloucester ▶

THEY THAT GO DOWN TO THE SEA IN SHIPS
1623 – 1923

INTERPRETING MAPS Over several days, three weather systems collided to create violent weather conditions. The first weather system was the low-pressure system that formed over the Great Lakes and moved east to Nova Scotia. The second system was the high-pressure system that formed over Quebec. The third system, Hurricane Grace, had formed over the Atlantic east of Florida.

▶ *Look at the air pressure map on page 148 again. Label the map with the number 1 where the first weather system formed, 2 for the second system, and 3 for the third system.*

READING A GRAPH

Water waves are usually caused by wind pushing the water in front of it. The graph at the right plots many measurements of wave height and wind speed during one year on Lake Michigan. Each plot looks like a circle. By reading the graph, you can see the wind speed and wave height when each measurement was taken.

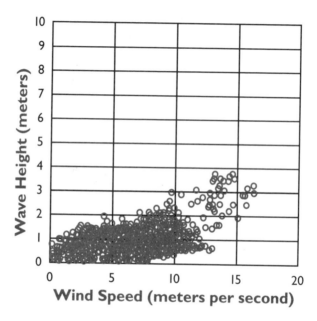

▶ *When wind speed was less than 5 meters per second, how high were most waves?*

_____

_____

▶ *What was the height of the tallest waves that were measured?*

_____

▶ *Did a wind speed of 10 m/s always produce waves of the same height? Explain your answer.*

_____

_____

_____

_____

Propose Explanations

UNDERSTANDING CAUSE AND EFFECT

▶ *What is the usual relationship between wind speed and wave height?*

_____

_____

Some buoys at sea automatically collect weather data. One buoy is very near the *Andrea Gail*'s last known position. By the evening of October 28, when the *Andrea Gail* was last heard from, the buoy was sending startling data. Wind speed was more than 100 miles (161 km) per hour. Waves were 70 feet (21 m) high. The *Andrea Gail* was lost at sea.

▶ *Based on what you've read, how do you think weather conditions might have caused the Andrea Gail to sink?*

_____

_____

_____

_____

Take Action

GENERATE QUESTIONS

▶ *You are investigating the disappearance of the Andrea Gail. What questions would you ask meteorologist Bob Case? What would you ask another swordfish boat captain? What would you ask the boat's builder? What would you ask a Coast Guard rescue officer?*

_____

_____

_____

_____

_____

_____

_____

_____

At Sea in a Storm

What do you do when your boat is filled with tens of thousands of dollars worth of fresh swordfish, your ice machine is failing, and a storm is on the way?

Sebastian Junger, author of *The Perfect Storm*, wondered about the same thing. As he wrote about the storm, Junger imagined what the captain of the *Andrea Gail* might have been thinking.

Of the many swordfishing boats at sea during "the perfect storm," only one—the *Andrea Gail*—sank in the storm. The tragic outcome was that captain Billy Tyne and his crew—Bugsy Moran, Dale Murphy, Alfred Pierre, Bobby Shatford, and David Sullivan—all lost their lives.

NOTEZONE

Underline the main reasons why the captain might have decided to head for home instead of sailing away from the storm.

 **Read**

Here's what Junger believes captain Billy Tyne was thinking.

The Perfect Storm

Billy finishes up his last haul around noon on the 25th and—the crew still stowing their gear—turns his boat for home. They'll be one of the only boats in port with a load of fish, which means a...high price.... Billy has a failing ice machine and a twelve hundred mile [1,900 km] drive ahead of him. He'll be heading in while the rest of the fleet is still in mid-trip....

Billy...has undoubtedly heard the forecast, but he's...[not] inclined to do anything about it.... Weather reports are vitally important to the fishing, but not so much for heading home. When the end of the trip comes, captains generally just haul their gear and go.

---

haul (noun): a load of fish that has been caught
stowing: putting away

inclined: willing
haul (verb): take aboard a boat

From: Junger, Sebastian. *The Perfect Storm: A True Story of Men Against the Sea.* Harper Collins.

▶ Explore

HEADING HOME This map shows the last known location of the *Andrea Gail* at 6 P.M. on October 28. After that, radio contact was lost. The boat and crew were never found.

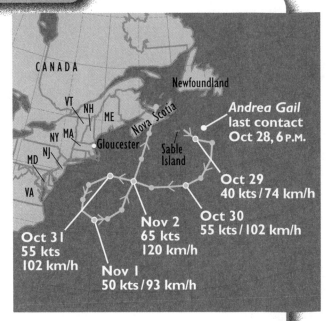

The *Andrea Gail* was heading to its home port of Gloucester on the coast of Massachusetts. Gloucester was almost 1,900 kilometers away.

▶ *What places were closer than Gloucester? Why do you think captain Billy Tyne didn't try to head there?*

_____

_____

_____

_____

The line on the map shows the path, or track, of "the perfect storm."

▶ *Do you think the **Andrea Gail** would have sailed into the storm as it tried to get home? Explain your answer.*

_____

_____

_____

UNDERSTANDING RISKS Captain Billy Tyne had heard the weather service forecasts. He knew that a violent storm was forming.

▶ *Why do you think he didn't drive his boat to the east, which is where the rest of the swordfishing boats waited out the storm?*

_____

_____

▶ *The crew and their families depended on the money made from the fish they caught. What risk did they face if the ice machine failed?*

_____

Down Tornado Alley

Tornado—coming to a cloudy sky near you!

Tornadoes are one of the deadliest forms of severe weather. Strong winds rushing into a funnel cloud can pull cars, livestock, and even buildings into the air and deposit them miles away.

▶ Before You Read

TORNADO WATCH Tornadoes can occur anywhere in the United States, but they're more likely to occur in some places than in others.

▶ *What would you do if you thought there might be a tornado heading toward your area? How would you find out for sure if a tornado was on the way?*

_____

_____

_____

_____

_____

_____

_____

_____

_____

_____

_____

UNIT 4: WEATHER AND CLIMATE

▶ Read

Here's 13-year-old Allen Nelson's report of a tornado that struck his town.

A SURVIVOR'S STORY

Name: Allen Nelson

Date: 13 September 1998

It was about September of this year when Hurricane Earl hit our middle-sized town of Orangeburg, South Carolina. All day at school (I'm 13 years old) there was horizontal rain and the clouds moved really fast. The wind was about 20 miles an hour ALL the time. I kept telling my friends, "I think there's gonna be a tornado." When I got home at about 4:00 that afternoon, there was a HUGE wall cloud hanging just a few miles from our house. All of a sudden the rain and wind stopped! I told my mom there's gonna be a tornado. I checked out the Weather Channel, and sure enough there was a tornado watch for our county! I put my books down and went back outside. I looked to the North East and there was a cloud of dust swirling! It dissipated, [but then] I saw another! Most of the dust clouds were white but I then looked to the west and saw a larger dust cloud and heard a slight buzzing or humming sound. I looked up at the cloud and saw a very small but well-developed funnel at the cloud base! I continued to watch, it [was] still forming and lengthening. Then, all at once, the funnel came and touched the ground! A tornado was born!

....

horizontal: sideways

wall cloud: a low-hanging cloud that rotates and can become a tornado

dissipated: broke up and disappeared

From: Nelson, Allen. "Twisters: Destruction From the Sky." *ThinkQuest.*
(tqjunior.thinkquest.org/4232/survivor.htm)

NOTEZONE

Underline all the words and phrases that describe the weather conditions associated with the tornado.

FIND OUT MORE

SCIENCESAURUS

Weather	218
Clouds	223
Wind	225

SCILINKS
THE WORLD'S A CLICK AWAY

INTERPRET A TORNADO MAP This map shows the average number of tornadoes that occur in different areas of the United States each year.

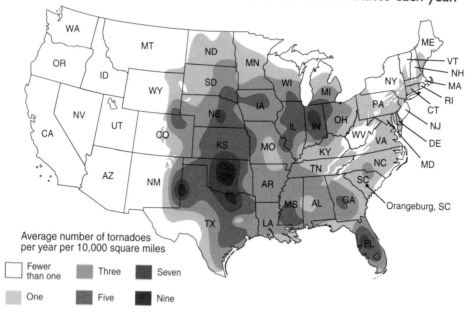

Average number of tornadoes per year per 10,000 square miles

☐ Fewer than one	
☐ One	
☐ Three	
◼ Five	
◼ Seven	
◼ Nine	

Orangeburg, SC

▶ **According to the map, which states have at least seven tornadoes per year?**

_____

_____

▶ **Which area of the country deserves the nickname "Tornado Alley"? Why?**

_____

_____

_____

▶ **How common are tornadoes in Orangeburg, South Carolina, where Allen Nelson lives?**

_____

_____

▶ **According to the map, how common are tornadoes where you live?**

_____

_____

Take Action

COMMUNICATE TORNADO SAFETY Would you know what to do if a tornado alert were broadcast for your area?

▶ Do some research to find out what you can do to be prepared for a tornado and what you should do during the tornado to be safe. Create a flier with a list of tornado safety rules. Add pictures to get your points across. Use the space below to plan your flier.

Weird Weather

Hail Hail!

How much damage can a ball of ice do? When it's falling from the sky at high speeds, a lot!

If you cut a hailstone in half, you'd see layers of ice. Each layer forms as the hailstone falls through a cloud, gathers water on its surface, and then is blown back high enough into the cloud for the water to freeze. Some hailstones are smaller than a pea. Others can be as large as golf balls—or even softballs! When the hailstones grow too large for the updrafts to lift them, they all start falling at once. So most hailstorms last only a few minutes.

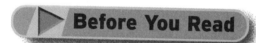 **Before You Read**

GENERATE IDEAS Imagine that you are riding in a car during a thunderstorm one summer day. Suddenly hail starts pounding down.

▶ *What might you observe around you? List your ideas.*

_____

_____

_____

_____

_____

_____

_____

_____

NOTEZONE

Underline the other states besides Colorado that have numerous, severe hailstorms.

Hail can cause millions of dollars in damage.

THE SUMMERTIME HAZARD OF EASTERN COLORADO

Hail—the word itself sends feelings of frustration through Colorado farmers. Each year, millions of dollars of agricultural losses occur when hailstorms sweep across the Eastern Plains. Hundreds of Colorado wheat farmers can tell tales of disappointment about years when their crop had survived drought, windstorms, winter cold, and insects only to be wiped out by hail the day before harvest. If it wasn't last year or the year before, then it might be this year or the next.

Hail is a pain, but it's also an unavoidable part of life east of the Rockies. All the way from Alberta, Canada, south to eastern New Mexico, hundreds (maybe thousands) of hailstorms develop each year. There is no other place in North America with more numerous or more severe hailstorms, and Colorado is right in the middle of it. There are areas in Wyoming, Montana, South Dakota, Nebraska and New Mexico that may challenge Colorado as the hail capital of the U.S., but more often than not, Colorado takes that honor.

....

agricultural: related to farming **numerous:** high in number
drought: a long period of dryness

From: Doesken, Nolan J. "Hail, Hail, Hail—The Summertime Hazard Of Eastern Colorado." *Colorado Climate.* Colorado Climate Center, Colorado State University. (ccc.atmos.colostate.edu/~hail/pdfs/Hail%20_Hazard.pdf)

FIND OUT MORE

SCIENCESAURUS
Water Cycle 216
Weather 218

▼ Wheat

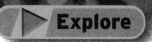

HAILSTONE SIZES Meteorologists depend on the reports of citizens for information on hailstorms. The histogram below shows the number of hailstorms and the sizes of hailstones reported in Colorado during a seven-year period.

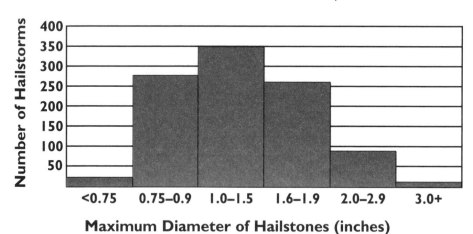

Severe Hailstorms in Colorado, 1986–1993

▶ *Which size hailstones were most often reported in Colorado?*

_____

▶ *Which size was least often reported?*

_____

▶ *The National Weather Service says that 95 percent of hailstorms involve hailstones less than 0.5 inches in diameter. What are some reasons why the bar for less than 0.75 inches is so short?*

_____

_____

_____

_____

_____

_____

_____

THINK ABOUT IT The hailstorm data in the graph is based on reports from people who call weather services and insurance companies to report hail falling in their area. Insurance companies will pay for damage on insured property caused by the weather.

▶ *Imagine you live and own property in Colorado. When would you report hail falling? Why? When would you not bother to report it? Why not?*

_____

_____

_____

Turn back to the tornado map on page 158. Use the information in the reading on page 161 to shade the states on the map that have a lot of hailstorms.

▶ *Which of those states also have an average of one or more tornadoes each year?*

_____

_____

Hailstorms and tornadoes both form out of severe thunderstorms.

▶ *What can you infer about the states that have both hailstorms and tornadoes?*

_____

_____

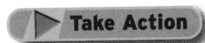

▶ Take Action

GENERATING QUESTIONS Make a list of questions about hailstorms that scientists could investigate—for example, *What weather conditions exist when hailstorms occur?* Think about ways that scientists could investigate these questions. Remember: Scientific questions must be testable.

_____

_____

_____

_____

DIGGING OUT

A fierce surprise snowstorm can leave people trapped indoors or stranded far from home.

A blizzard is not just your average snowstorm. It's a severe storm with high wind speeds, temperatures well below freezing, and snow falling fast enough to make seeing difficult. The snow piles up rapidly and gets so high that it can take days to clear away. In one of the most famous storms, the blizzard of 1888, more than 400 people lost their lives.

NOTEZONE

Underline the words that explain why no one expected the storm.

 **Read**

A man living in Connecticut when the blizzard hit remembered the storm 50 years later.

The Blizzard of 1888

I couldn't see ten feet ahead of me... Snow was up to my waist. It kept snowin' all day Tuesday, and Wednesday...when I went up to town there was a drift way over your head clear from the town hall across to Woodruff's house.

Warren Westwood and Bill Woods, who...used to drive... [a horse-drawn wagon]...to work...started out Monday noon. They bought a snow shovel.... They got stuck in a big drift miles from home. One of them got the horse out and got on his back and the other took hold of the horse's tail. They hadn't got very far this way when the horse dropped dead. They plodded on, makin' their way the best they could by what landmarks they could recognize. They climbed over stone walls, and dead trees, and fell down I don't know how many times, and they was near exhausted.

...That was the worst snowstorm there ever was. And it was such beautiful weather before—nobody could realize what was comin'.

plodded: walked slowly   **landmark:** an object that marks a location

From: "Weatherlore." *Federal Writers' Project.* Library of Congress.

FIND OUT MORE

SCIENCESAURUS
Water Cycle	216
Weather	218

UNIT 4: WEATHER AND CLIMATE

▶ Propose Explanations

COMPARE AND CONTRAST

What tools did people use to clear the snow from the blizzard of 1888? Look for clues in the reading and in the photograph.

▼1888: Snow removal in Connecticut

_____

_____

▶ **What tools do we have today for clearing large amounts of snow?**

_____

_____

▶ **How do people today find out about blizzards that are on the way? Why couldn't people be warned about the coming blizzard in 1888?**

_____

_____

_____

_____

_____

_____

MAKE INFERENCES

▶ **How did the tools available in 1888 affect how well people could clear the snow from the storm?**

_____

_____

_____

Climate Change

Ancient Climates

What can ancient trees tell us about ancient climates? A lot.

Climate is the average weather conditions—temperature and precipitation—in a particular place over a long period of time. Scientists are trying to find out if climates around the world are changing. They need to compare conditions in recent years with conditions hundreds and even thousands of years ago. One way to do this is to study ancient trees.

▶ **Redwood forest**

Trees that live in areas with seasonal changes form growth rings in their trunks. Each year a new ring forms. The thickness of a ring depends on the weather conditions during the year it formed—thicker rings in wet weather and thinner rings in dry weather. Over a tree's lifetime, the rings form a year-by-year record of the climate. *Dendrochronology* is the study of how tree ring patterns relate to climate changes in the past.

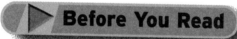 **Before You Read**

INSIDE A TREE Have you ever looked at the end of a log that had been sawed straight across? Draw what the inside of the tree trunk looked like.

▶ Read

NOTEZONE

Underline the procedure that the scientists used to produce a growth record.

Fidel Roig found thousands of years of climate data in ancient South American tree stumps.

What Trees Know

Fifty millennia ago, volcanic ash and mud buried a forest of conifers along a Pacific shoreline in what is now southern Chile. Now, by examining the tree rings of the remaining stumps, an international team of scientists has reconstructed the earliest year-to-year record yet of climate [conditions].

The stumps of the tree species *Fitzroya cupressoides* are roughly 50,000 years old, says lead scientist Fidel A. Roig.... Data from these trees "provide a year-by-year indication of general climate [patterns]...," says team member Keith R. Briffa.... Using annual growth-ring patterns in trees, some researchers have inferred temperatures dating back about 10,000 years, or to the end of the last ice age....

In the new analysis...scientists took cross sections of 28 of the ancient stumps and measured the width of each tree ring. By averaging the data, they produced a growth record of the 1,229 years before the trees were buried, the researchers say....

Connie A. Woodhouse, a paleoclimatologist...cautions that the new data provide only a "snapshot" of an ancient climate. She says she hopes researchers will uncover more trees that can bridge the gap between old and new climate records.

conifer: a tree that has needle-like leaves and produces seeds in cones
reconstructed: built something again

ice age: a time period when Earth's climate was cooler and sheets of ice covered large areas of land
paleoclimatologist: a scientist who studies ancient climates

From: Wang, Linda. "Ancient Tree Rings Reveal Past Climate." *Science News*.

FIND OUT MORE

SCIENCESAURUS
Climate   227
Factors Affecting
   Climate   228
Pattern of World
   Climates   230

SCILINKS
THE WORLD'S A CLICK AWAY

www.scilinks.org
Keyword: Changes in
   Climate
Code: GSED20

HOW ARE DATA COLLECTED? A tree trunk grows in circumference each growing season. How much it grows depends on conditions such as temperature, rainfall, and sunlight. For example, a tree grows more in a rainy year than in a dry year. A ring forms as each growing season comes and goes. While the tree is growing quickly, a light-colored band of new growth forms. When growth slows later in the growing season, a darker color band forms.

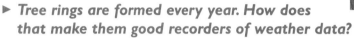

▶ *Tree rings are formed every year. How does that make them good recorders of weather data?*

_____

_____

Scientists also collect samples of an ancient tree's rings by drilling sideways into the trunk and removing a core sample. The sample contains a small piece of every ring. They measure and record the width of each ring.

▶ *Suppose scientists see a thicker growth ring for one year than for others. What can they infer about weather conditions that year?*

_____

_____

By studying the core sample of a tree that lived 50,000 years ago, scientists can make a year-by-year time line of weather conditions during the lifetime of the tree. (This core sample is labeled number 1 in the diagram.) Scientists also take core samples of other ancient tree stumps—some older, some younger—in the same area. (These core samples are numbered 2 and 3 in the diagram.) They then compare the ring patterns from all the samples by overlapping their matching rings. This method provides a longer time line than only one tree can provide.

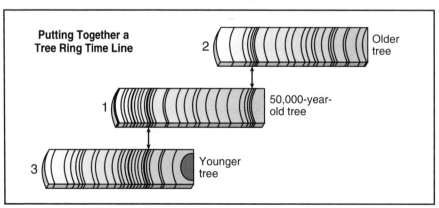

Putting Together a Tree Ring Time Line

2 — Older tree

1 — 50,000-year-old tree

3 — Younger tree

► What evidence would scientists need in order to infer that the climate had changed in an area over a thousand years?

_____

_____

_____

_____

_____

READING TREES A tree's growth is affected by many factors. These include soil moisture, air and soil temperatures, sunlight, and wind. Insect attacks and forest fires also affect tree growth. The width of a tree ring is the result of all these factors. For some trees, one factor may be more important than the others. If a ring is thick or thin, the dendrochronologist can infer what weather condition may have caused it.

Trees on high mountains, where it is cold, are most affected by changes in temperature. In warmer years with enough soil moisture, the trees will grow more. In colder years with the same soil moisture, they will grow less.

► What climate condition could dendrochronologists study by observing rings from trees on a mountaintop? What characteristic of the rings would provide evidence of warmer or cooler years?

_____

_____

► What climate condition could dendrochronologists study by taking core samples from trees in dry, hot, desert-like areas?

_____

_____

▶ Take Action

DO RESEARCH Climate scientists find weather records in other places besides tree rings. Find out about one of the following. What makes it a good recorder of climate change?

- glacier ice
- fossil pollen
- ocean sediments
- ocean coral

Climate Change

ON THIN ICE

Climate change may have the greatest effect on people who depend on ice.

The Inuit people live in Arctic Canada and in Alaska. Here, in one of the harshest climates on Earth, the Inuit build homes, gather food, and raise families. Their traditional diet includes fish, seals, and other mammals. Sometimes whales are hunted. Seals are the Inuit's main food source during the winter. Seals also provide food for their dogs, skins for clothing, tents, and boats, and fuel for light and heat.

▲ Inuit girl

The Inuit hunt seals on the Arctic Ocean ice. But lately, hunting is more dangerous than in the past. This is because the ice is thin in places where the Inuit had safely hunted seals for generations.

Read

NOTEZONE

Underline the evidence of unusually warm weather that has been observed by the Inuit people.

FIND OUT MORE

SCIENCESAURUS

Climate 227
Factors Affecting Climate 228
Pattern of World Climates 230

SCILINKS.
THE WORLD'S A CLICK AWAY

www.scilinks.org
Keyword: Changes in Climate
Code: GSED20

Reporter Sue Armstrong visited a Canadian Inuit village in 2001. Here she describes some of the changes the villagers have been experiencing.

ARCTIC CHANGES

Unusual events are being reported across the Arctic. Inuit families going off on snowmobiles to prepare their summer hunting camps have found themselves cut off from home by a sea of mud, following early thaws. Some have discovered that the meat they cached in the ice as food for future trips has thawed and rotted. There are reports of igloos losing their insulating properties as the snow drips and refreezes; of caribou clothing clogging with ice in unusually humid weather; of lakes draining into the sea as permafrost melts...and sea ice breaking up earlier than usual, carrying seals beyond the reach of hunters.

cached: stored in a hidden place
igloo: a temporary Inuit home made from blocks of solid snow
insulating: keeping heat in or out

permafrost: a layer of permanently frozen soil below the ground's surface

From: Armstrong, Sue. "Climate Change." *New Scientist.* (www.newscientist.com/hottopics/climate/climate.jsp?id=23154500)

UNIT 4: WEATHER AND CLIMATE

► Explore

PREDICTING CHANGE Think about the unusual events reported by the Inuit.

► *How might the Arctic climate be changing?*

_____

_____

► *How do you think this change could affect the Inuit way of life?*

_____

_____

_____

_____

_____

CONTRIBUTING TO SCIENCE With their traditions in danger, Inuit people are thinking ahead about possible climate change. Elders in Nunavut, Canada, meet to make plans for dealing with the changes. They are also sharing their lifelong knowledge of Arctic climate with scientists.

Children in Nunavut schools are also helping scientists. With their teachers, they collect weather data and check snow and ice conditions. They also record when buds open on certain plants and when insect eggs hatch. Hatching and budding are partly determined by air temperature.

► *If students and scientists find that insects in the same place are hatching earlier year after year, what might that tell them about the climate?*

_____

_____

Climate Change

MELTDOWN?

Global warming is melting Arctic sea ice. Or is it?

You've probably heard the term *global warming*. Global warming is the idea that the average worldwide air temperature has risen over the past 100 years. Because air temperature is a major factor in climate, global warming may be changing climates around the world. Climate scientists are especially interested in the Arctic. Here, in the land of ice and snow, small increases in temperature can cause big changes.

▶ Before You Read

LOCAL CLIMATE Write about the climate and seasonal changes where you live.

▶ *How many hours of daylight do you have in winter? How many in summer? Is there more precipitation in one season, or is precipitation about the same all year? Does the average temperature change during the year? What is the highest average temperature? What is the lowest?*

_____

_____

_____

_____

_____

_____

_____

_____

_____

UNIT 4: WEATHER AND CLIMATE

NOTEZONE

Underline the
two ideas
scientists have
for why the
ice is thinning.

Some scientists hypothesize that global warming is reducing the amount of ice in the Arctic. Other scientists disagree.

Melting Above, Melting Below

The great ice cover that stretches across the top of the globe has become about 40 percent thinner than it was two to four decades ago, scientists have found after analyzing data collected by nuclear submarines....

The scientists found...that from 1958 through 1976, the average thickness of the Arctic sea ice was about 10 feet [3 meters]. From 1993 through 1997, it was about six feet [1.8 meters]. In the 1990's, say the researchers, the thinning appeared to be continuing at a rate of about four inches [10 cm] a year.

There is substantial evidence that the climate of the Arctic and sub-Arctic region is warming, at least in some seasons. The area covered by sea ice has diminished and the duration of the cover has shortened in many places. Mountain glaciers in Alaska have shrunk, as has the Greenland ice cap.

The average surface temperature of the earth has risen by about 1 degree Fahrenheit [17 degrees Celsius] or a little more over the last century and by several times that amount in northern regions.

[Some scientists think] that a shift in ...natural patterns of atmospheric circulation in the Arctic may be responsible for the warmer North and the thinning sea ice. Other scientists say that the shift in natural patterns may have been touched off or enhanced by global warming....

---

substantial: a lot of
diminished: lessened
duration: how long something lasts
ice cap: ice and snow that cover a large area

atmospheric circulation: the movement of air masses in Earth's atmosphere
global warming: an increase in the world's average temperature, possibly caused in part by fossil fuel use

From: Stevens, William K. "Thinning Sea Ice Stokes Debate on Climate Debate." *The New York Times.*

SCI**LINKS**
THE WORLD'S A CLICK AWAY

www.scilinks.org
Keyword: Changes
 in Climate
Code: GSED20

173

DISTINGUISHING DATA FROM CONCLUSIONS

DISTINGUISHING DATA FROM CONCLUSIONS Scientists disagree about if and why Arctic ice is changing. Some scientists argue that conclusions are being drawn when there are not enough observations to support them.

▶ *Based on what you learned in the reading, label each of the following sentences "observation" or "conclusion."*

Sentence	Observation or Conclusion?
Air temperatures during some seasons in the Arctic have risen.	
The average thickness of Arctic sea ice has decreased since 1958.	
Global warming is causing a shift in natural climate patterns.	
Arctic ice is thinning because of natural climate patterns.	
Arctic ice showed 40% thinning in the last 2 to 4 decades.	
Global warming is causing the Arctic sea ice to melt.	

ANALYZING VARIABLES

▶ *How might when the data were collected affect the results?*

_____

_____

▶ *How might where the data were collected affect the results?*

_____

_____

 **Propose Explanations**

EVALUATE CONCLUSIONS Greg Holloway is a scientist at the Institute of Ocean Studies in Canada. He doesn't believe there's a "big melt" in the Arctic sea. He says not enough data have been collected to draw conclusions. The submarines that took the ice thickness data, for example, looked at only a small part of the Arctic sea. Holloway thinks winds may have pushed the ice into Canadian waters for a time. The submarines never entered Canadian waters. He thinks the ice may be becoming thicker in some spots and thinner in others—but is not disappearing.

▶ *Why is it too soon to draw the following conclusion?* Global warming is causing the total volume of Arctic ice to decrease.

_____

_____

_____

_____

_____

_____

_____

▶ *List questions you'd like answered in order to be sure about changes in Arctic ice.*

_____

_____

_____

_____

_____

_____

_____

 **Take Action**

WRITE A RESEARCH PROPOSAL Pick one of the questions you listed above. Then, on a separate sheet of paper, develop a proposal to research the question. Your proposal should include the following parts.

1. The question you want to answer
2. The data you plan to collect
3. How you will go about collecting the data
4. Why having the data is important

UNIT 5 Astronomy

How do astronomers study objects in space?

When scientists want to learn about rocks or fossils, they can just dig into Earth's surface. But even the astronomers at NASA have to think up creative methods when it comes to approaching the sky.

In this unit you'll learn about objects in space and the tools scientists use to study them. Astronomers try to predict the orbit of a comet or asteroid when it approaches Earth and are even using probes to analyze the material in a comet's tail! They have debated whether Pluto is really a planet, have discovered evidence of water on Mars in the distant past, and have analyzed what the moons in our solar system are made of. You'll also learn about the life cycles of stars and the search for planets beyond our own solar system. And finally, you'll examine the "how" and "why" of space exploration.

? Did You Know?

In a nearby solar system, our sun has
what might be considered a "cousin"
star named Epsilon Eridani. In orbit
around the star is a very large planet
with characteristics similar to Earth's.
Scientists wonder whether this newly
discovered planet might support life.

Rocks and Ice in Orbit

Close Encounters

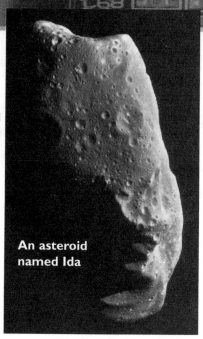

As we go about our daily lives, giant rocks are whirling around in space. Some are a little too close for comfort.

Scientists theorize that the solar system formed when a huge cloud of gases and dust came together. As these bits of material crashed into one another, they became larger and larger. Most of the dust and gas joined to form the sun. Most of the rest of the material eventually formed the planets, but there were leftover pieces.

An asteroid named Ida

If you could travel in a spaceship between the planets Mars and Jupiter, you might run into some leftover pieces—big rocky ones called *asteroids*. Asteroids are chunks of rock that are too small to be called planets. The area between Mars and Jupiter is called the Asteroid Belt because it contains most of our solar system's asteroids. A few asteroids, however, are closer to the sun than the Asteroid Belt. Like planets, asteroids travel around the sun along paths called *orbits*. The orbits of both asteroids and planets are ellipses (ovals) rather than circles. Asteroids' orbits usually are longer ellipses than planets' orbits. Scientists are interested in predicting the orbits of asteroids they find in space. Can you guess why?

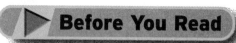

▶ Before You Read

ROUND AND ROUND The drawing below shows the orbit of Earth around the sun. On the same drawing, show what you think the orbit of an asteroid might look like.

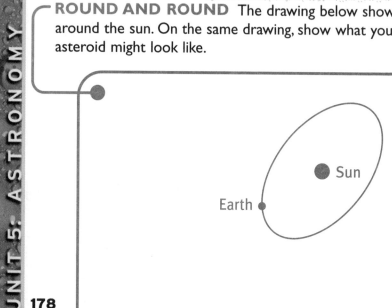

Sun

Earth

UNIT 5: ASTRONOMY

Read

NOTEZONE

Underline the reason why an asteroid might not be noticed as it approached Earth.

In March of 2002, Earth had a near miss with a passing asteroid.

Asteroid Passes Near Earth

An asteroid large enough to demolish a medium-sized city passed within 288,000 miles [460,800 km] of Earth without being noticed by astronomers until four days later.

The asteroid, about 165 feet [49.5 m] across, came from the direction of the sun, making it difficult for astronomers to spot. It passed by Earth on March 8, but wasn't seen until March 12 as it hurtled away.

Gareth Williams of the International Astronomical Union's Minor Planet Center in Cambridge, Massachusetts, helped spot the asteroid after it passed by. It was a close call in space terms. The moon is only 250,000 miles [400,00 km] away.

▲ A telescope in New Mexico

"The key is to detect these objects before they come out of the (sun's direction)," Williams told the Florida Today newspaper in Wednesday editions.

That way, astronomers can quickly determine an asteroid's orbit and predict whether it will hit the Earth.

....

astronomer: a scientist who studies the objects in space

From: *The Associated Press.* March 20, 2002.

FIND OUT MORE

SCIENCESAURUS

Solar System
  Objects   238
Asteroids   241

COMPARE ASTEROID ORBITS Astronomers around the world keep track of asteroids like the one in the reading. Once they have discovered an asteroid, the next step is to try to predict its orbit. Astronomers know that an asteroid's orbit is in the shape of an ellipse. They also know that the ellipse lies in an imaginary flat surface called a plane. The trick is to figure out the exact size and length of the ellipse and the angle of its plane. How do scientists do that? They use a strategy that you use to solve some math problems—estimate and check.

Astronomers begin by estimating the path the asteroid might follow and predicting its position in the sky. They then make observations of the asteroid's actual position in the sky as seen from Earth.

This diagram shows an imaginary asteroid's predicted position and its actual position. This imaginary asteroid has its orbit in the same plane as Earth. Most real asteroids would have an orbit in a different plane.

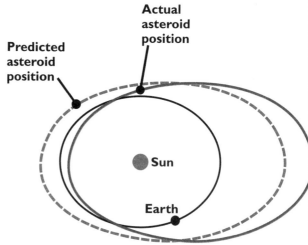

Sizes not to scale

▶ *If the asteroid's predicted position and its actual position are not the same, what might astronomers conclude about their prediction?*

_____

▶ *If the asteroid's predicted position and actual position are not the same, what step must astronomers take next?*

_____

_____

_____

▶ *How will the astronomers know if their new prediction of the asteroid's orbit is correct?*

_____

_____

▶ *Mark an X on the diagram to show the places where the actual orbit of the asteroid crosses Earth's orbit.*

180

WHY PREDICT ASTEROID ORBITS?

▶ *How can astronomers predict future positions of an asteroid?*

_____

_____

_____

▶ *Why would people on Earth be interested in the orbits of asteroids, especially those that are closer than the Asteroid Belt?*

_____

_____

_____

_____

▶ *Look again at the actual orbit of the imaginary asteroid in the diagram. Where in its orbit would the asteroid have to be to collide with Earth? Where would Earth have to be?*

_____

_____

_____

_____

_____

_____

_____

Take Action

DRAW A DIAGRAM On a sheet of graph paper, draw a diagram that shows the positions of Earth, the moon, and the asteroid as described in the reading. Use a scale for distance of 1 square = 10,000 km. Show the asteroid's position when it passed Earth. Label the distance between Earth and the asteroid when it passed.

Rocks and Ice in Orbit

OFF TRACK

Hubble NASA images

Comet LINEAR fragments

One giant snowball threw astronomers for a loop.

Most scientists believe that comets, like asteroids, are bits of material left over from the early days of our solar system. While asteroids are mostly rock, comets are made of dust, rock, and ice. Comets travel in large orbits that stretch to the far reaches of the solar system. As their orbits take them closer to the sun, they give off gases and rock particles. These materials often form comet tails that can be seen from Earth.

Astronomers can predict the orbits of comets, just as they can predict the orbits of asteroids. But comets are more likely than asteroids to "jump" orbit and move in a new direction. A comet named LINEAR did this. Comet LINEAR is named after the Lincoln Near-Earth Asteroid Research program. Astronomers in this program discovered LINEAR in September 1999.

 Read

LINEAR was a surprising comet. Here is its story.

A Comet Changes Course

August 11, 2000

The astronomers measured LINEAR's movements in the sky. Using the measurements, they calculated just how they thought LINEAR would travel around the sun. But as LINEAR got closer to the sun, it didn't follow its expected path. It still hurtled toward the sun, but it dodged this way and that as it went.

The reason LINEAR bounced around so much is that a comet [is] like a "dirty snowball" [made of dust, rock, and ice]. As a comet travels in from the outer reaches of the solar system, the sun heats it.

FIND OUT MORE

SCIENCESAURUS

Solar System
  Objects   238
  Comets   242

SCILINKS.
THE WORLD'S A CLICK AWAY
www.scilinks.org
Keywords: Comets,
  Asteroids, and Meteors
Code: GSED21

UNIT 5: ASTRONOMY

When the ice in a comet is heated quickly, it can turn to a gas suddenly. The gases shoot outward, and can move the comet just like small rocket motors. LINEAR is small for a comet, about the size of a mountain. So these jets of gas, and chunks of rocks breaking off, were able to push LINEAR off course.

...But the final surprise came when LINEAR passed close to the sun.... The sun's heat was enough to cause LINEAR to blow apart in an explosion.... Astronomers believe that most comets eventually just disintegrate and disappear. LINEAR was just more spectacular than most!

NOTEZONE

Underline the sentences that explain what caused LINEAR to move off course.

hurtled: sped
dodged: moved from side to side
outer reaches: the places in the solar system that are the farthest away from the sun, beyond Neptune and Pluto
disintegrate: fall apart into tiny pieces

From: "Comet Meltdown!." *NASA Kids.* Center Operations Directorate at Marshall Space Flight Center. (kids.msfc.nasa.gov/news/2000/news%2Dlinear.asp)

▶ Propose Explanations

▶ **What materials are comets made of?**

_____

▶ **Why do these materials make small comets more likely to change course than asteroids, which are made mostly of rock?**

_____

_____

_____

_____

▶ **What do you suppose might have caused the great explosion of comet LINEAR? (Hint: Think about the gas and the pressure it produces.)**

_____

_____

_____

Rocks and Ice in Orbit

Capturing Comet Dust

What's the best way to study a comet? Go and get a piece of it!

Astronomers think comets have changed little since they first formed at the same time as the rest of the solar system. For this reason, comets may be able to teach us about the history of the solar system. They may also contain materials like those that formed the early planets. But how can we study a comet up close?

◀ **StarDust probe**

 Before You Read

LONG WAY HOME Sometimes taking the "long way" is the best way to get to where you are going. Think of a time when traveling a longer distance made your trip easier or better. It might have been when you were walking, cycling, or even riding a bus.

▶ *Describe how the trip was longer and why this was better than taking the "short way."*

_____

_____

_____

_____

_____

_____

▶ Read

Here's NASA's plan to get a first look at actual comet material.

STARDUST

NASA is using relatively simple low-cost probes to explore our solar system. Launched in February 1999 on a small Delta rocket, the StarDust probe will intercept and analyze the contents of a comet's tail, take close-up pictures, and then for the first time return its "catch" to Earth for complete analysis.

The mission will take a long 7 years, but by being patient, the total cost of the mission is reduced dramatically. Taking advantage of Earth's gravitational field, the craft will require a lot less...rocket fuel, and a smaller rocket can be used. After its first trip around the sun, StarDust's cleverly designed trajectory will loop it back toward Earth allowing Earth's gravitational field to slingshot the craft toward comet...Wild-2 (pronounced "vilt").

In January 2004...StarDust will finally catch up to comet Wild-2 and come within 100 kilometers of the comet's nucleus.

After another 1 billion-mile [1.6 billion-km] trip back to Earth, [part of] StarDust will...reenter Earth's atmosphere in January 2006 and parachute safely down onto the desert in the western United States.... Scientists will then be able to study the cometary... materials.... Hopefully, these studies will give us important clues about the evolution of the solar system and the origins of life on Earth.

---

probes: instruments used to collect data

intercept: move into

gravitational field: the force that pulls objects toward Earth and keeps them in orbit around it

trajectory: the path of a body or object through space

slingshot: in space science, using gravity to gain speed

nucleus: the solid part of a comet

cometary: related to comets

FIND OUT MORE

SCIENCESAURUS

Solar System
Objects   238
Comets   242

From: "Stardust." *Liftoff. Science@NASA.* Marshall Space Flight Center.
(liftoff.msfc.nasa.gov/academy/space/solarsystem/comets/stardust.html)

INTERPRET A DIAGRAM

This diagram shows StarDust's three orbits of the sun as the probe travels along its journey.

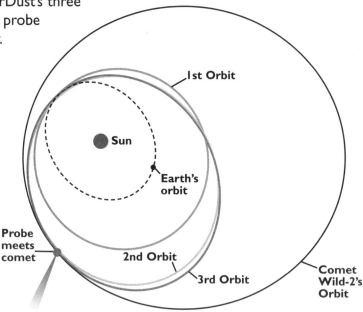

▶ *How is the comet's orbit different from Earth's orbit?*

_____

_____

_____

As StarDust finishes its first orbit, astronomers use remote controls to change the probe's flight path. This slight change brings the probe closer to Earth. As it flies by, the probe gets a boost from Earth's gravitational field.

▶ *Look at StarDust's second orbit around the sun. How does this boost affect StarDust's orbit?*

_____

_____

▶ *How are NASA astronomers using Earth's gravitational field to reduce the cost of the StarDust project?*

_____

_____

_____

THINK ABOUT IT Astronomers are excited about studying the materials found in comets.

▶ *What might they be able to learn about the solar system that they couldn't learn by studying materials here on Earth? Explain your answer. (Hint: How might Earth materials have changed over billions of years? How have comet materials changed, according to scientists?)*

_____

_____

_____

_____

WATCHING COMET BITS AND PIECES Space probes aren't the only way to observe pieces of comets. On certain nights of the year, you can just go outside and look up at the sky. For example, every October bits of Halley's Comet streak through the sky. You can see them if you live in a place with dark skies, away from city lights.

As a comet's orbit brings it near the sun, it gives off gases and rock particles. Many of the particles stay in the same orbit as the comet. As Earth crosses the part of the comet's orbit where these particles are located, the particles enter Earth's atmosphere. There they burn up in many streaks of light that can be seen on a clear night. This event is called a meteor shower.

▶ *The diagram shows the orbits of Earth and Halley's Comet. Mark the points where it might be possible to see a meteor shower made of bits of this comet.*

Earth

orbit of
Halley's Comet

Sun

▶ *How many times each year would you expect a meteor shower from Halley's Comet? Explain.*

_____

▶ *A space probe is one way to observe comet dust. Explain how and when an aircraft could also observe bits of comets up close.*

_____

_____

_____

_____

187

Solar System News

PLANET STATUS

Is Pluto a planet or a comet? Does it matter?

Our solar system is full of objects. Some are large, some are small, some are rocky, and some are just big balls of gas. But one thing all these objects share is that they constantly orbit the sun. These objects include planets such as Earth and Mars and smaller bodies such as comets and asteroids.

Since its discovery in 1930, Pluto has been classified as a planet—the smallest and most distant planet in our solar system. But recently scientists debated whether or not Pluto should be classified as a planet. When the American Museum of Natural History in New York City opened its new space center, the exhibits did not mention Pluto as a planet. What's all the fuss about?

▲ **Kitt Peak National Observatory in Arizona**

Before You Read

WHAT IS A PLANET?
▶ *Create your own definition of a planet.*

_____

_____

_____

_____

_____

_____

_____

▶ Read

NoteZone

Underline the reason why news reports incorrectly said Pluto was to be demoted to a Minor Planet or a Trans-Neptunian Object.

Pluto no longer a planet? The idea had many people defending our smallest and oddest planet.

Long Live Planet Pluto!

It's official: Pluto is still a planet, and [no one will] change that anytime soon.

The ruling by the world's leading astronomical organization came [during] a brewing cosmic storm among scientists and stargazers, afraid that the smallest planet in the solar system was being demoted. News reports had said Pluto was to be demoted to a Minor Planet, or worse, a Trans-Neptunian Object. That simply isn't so, the International Astronomical Union [IAU] said. "No proposal to change the status of Pluto as the ninth planet in the solar system has been made by...the IAU...," said the 80-year-old organization, the final authority on astronomical matters....

Discussions have been under way on creating a [possible] numbering system for Trans-Neptunian Objects, and giving Pluto a number, too. These objects, which are beyond Neptune in the outer solar system, have some similarities to Pluto such as the type of orbit.... Including Pluto in a cataloging system would [help] the study of such objects.... "The discussion was [the same as] giving Pluto a social security number," [said] IAU Secretary-General Johannes Andersen.... "But other people saw it as a sort of attack on Pluto as a planet."

▼ Image of Pluto made by NASA

astronomical: related to the study of objects in space
cosmic: related to the universe
demoted: brought down in rank
Trans-Neptunian: located outside planet Neptune's orbit around the sun
proposal: suggestion
cataloging: identifying and listing

From: "Long Live Planet Pluto!" *The Associated Press.*

FIND OUT MORE

SCIENCESAURUS

Solar System	
Objects	238
Planets	240

SCI LINKS
THE WORLD'S A CLICK AWAY

www.scilinks.org
Keyword: The Nine Planets
Code: GSED22

WHAT'S IN A NAME? When Pluto was discovered in 1930, it was added to the list of planets as the ninth in our solar system. Like other planets, Pluto orbits the sun, has a rounded shape, and has weather and seasons. It is made of solid rock and ice. It also has a moon named Charon, which is half its size.

But Pluto is much smaller than the other planets in the solar system. It is even smaller than some of the moons. Its orbit is a longer oval than the other planets' orbits. Also, as you can see in the diagram, Pluto's orbit is on a different plane from those of the other planets. In these ways, Pluto is like a comet or asteroid.

Read the following definitions of a planet and a comet.

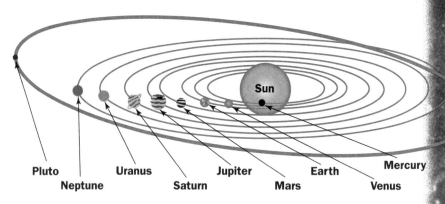

Pluto   Uranus   Jupiter   Earth   Mercury
  Neptune   Saturn   Mars   Venus

Planet: A body in the solar system that is larger than several meters in diameter, does not produce large amounts of heat (like a star), and orbits only the sun (not another body). A planet can be mostly rock, or it can have an outer layer of gases. A planet can have its own orbiting body—a moon. Most planets have moons much smaller than they are.

Comet: A small body of rock, dust, and ice that orbits the sun in a highly oval path. Comets' orbits are very oval and not in the same plane as the planets' orbits. The diameter of the solid part of a comet is only about 15 kilometers.

MAKE A GRAPHIC ORGANIZER

▶ *Is Pluto more like a planet or a comet? Create a graphic organizer below to help you answer the question.*

Pluto

Propose Explanations

APPLYING KNOWLEDGE

▶ *Why do you think scientists disagree over how to classify Pluto?*

_____

_____

_____

▶ *The reading says a "cosmic storm" erupted when people thought Pluto was being demoted to a Trans-Neptunian Object. Why might people care about Pluto's classification?*

_____

_____

_____

▶ *Do you think scientists should be influenced by what the public thinks about Pluto's classification? Why or why not?*

_____

_____

_____

Take Action

INVENT A MNEMONIC A mnemonic is a word clue that helps you remember some other information. To help remember the order and names of the nine planets in our solar system, many people use the mnemonic **M**y **V**ery **E**ducated **M**other **J**ust **S**erved **U**s **N**ine **P**izzas (**M**ercury **V**enus **E**arth **M**ars **J**upiter **S**aturn **U**ranus **N**eptune **P**luto).

▶ *Make up as many new mnemonics as you can think of to help you remember the order and names of the nine planets.*

_____

_____

_____

_____

_____

Solar System News

martian Water

Did Mars once have lots of water? Scientists are beginning to think so.

When you look at Mars with binoculars or a telescope, the planet's surface appears reddish in color. You can even see the reddish color when you look at Mars at night with your naked eye. For this reason, people in the past have nick-named Mars "the Red Planet."

Scientists have studied Mars for years. From what they could tell, the planet is very dry, like a desert. There is little moisture in its atmosphere. A closer look at the Martian surface, however, suggests that Mars might not always have been as dry as it is today.

▲ Mars

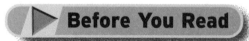 **Before You Read**

PUDDLE JUMPING Think about an area of bare soil near your home or school where there are no plants growing. How could you tell if the area was covered by puddles recently or if rainwater has run over its surface? Describe or draw your ideas below.

Read

Scientists study photographs of Mars's surface for clues about how the planet has changed since it formed billions of years ago.

The Case of the Missing Mars Water

Mars may once have been a very wet place. A [lot] of clues remain from an earlier era, billions of years ago, hinting that the Red Planet [had] great rivers, lakes, and perhaps even an ocean. But some of the clues are contradictory....

Based on what we have observed so far, Mars today is a frozen desert. It's too cold for liquid water to exist on its surface and too cold to rain. The planet's atmosphere is also too thin to permit any significant amount of snowfall.

...But there must have been water, and plenty of it, in Mars's past. That is evident from the massive [water] channels that are found [there]....

...Where has all that water gone? Was it absorbed into the ground where it remains today, frozen? Or [was it] lost to space? No one knows for certain.

In 2003, NASA will send two rovers to Mars to hunt for [signs of water] in rocks and soil on the surface. But many questions about the history of water on Mars are likely to remain unanswered until samples are returned from the Red Planet for examination on Earth.

FIND OUT MORE

SCIENCESAURUS
Solar System
  Objects   238
Planets   240

▼ **Martian landscape**

era: a period of time in history
contradictory: saying things that are the opposite of each other
atmosphere: the layer of gases above a planet's surface
significant: fairly large
evident: easily seen

massive: huge
channel: a trench or groove left by flowing water
rover: a vehicle that can move around to collect data on the surface of a planet

From: "The Case of the Missing Mars Water." *Science@NASA*. Marshall Space Flight Center. (science.nasa.gov/headlines/y2001/ast05jan_1.htm)

INTERPRET A SCIENTIFIC IMAGE This image of Mars's surface was taken by a camera aboard the *Viking Orbiter*—a spacecraft that orbited Mars in the late 1970s. Look closely at the different landforms in the picture. Use the line at the top of the image to get an idea of the size of the area you are looking at.

▶ *List your observations of the image. Describe what you see as clearly as possible.*

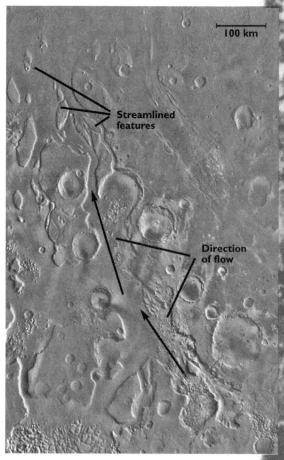

_____

_____

_____

_____

_____

_____

_____

_____

_____

_____

_____

_____

_____

_____

The circles on the surface are impact craters that formed when rocks from space hit Mars. All craters are round when they are first formed. But forces such as running water acting on the surface of the planet can change their shape.

▶ *What do you notice about some of the craters near the center of the image? Are they full circles?*

_____

_____

_____

_____

► *How does the texture of the surface vary in the image? Which parts appear rough? Which parts look smooth? What differences do you notice?*

_____

_____

_____

_____

Propose Explanations

MAKE INFERENCES Scientists who studied this image of Mars's surface compared the patterns they saw with patterns they observe on Earth's surface. Then they used the comparison to make inferences about forces acting on Mars's surface.

► *What processes do you think could have changed the shape of the craters in the middle of the image? (Hint: Think about the processes and actions here on Earth that move dirt around.)*

_____

_____

► *What conclusions might you draw about how the different textures seen in the picture were created? (Hint: Think about the processes you just identified.)*

_____

_____

Take Action

MISSION TO MARS Imagine that you and two classmates are going to be the first astronauts ever to walk on the surface of Mars. How would you investigate the history of water on the planet? What clues would you look for on the surface? Where else might you look for clues? (Hint: Think about the sorts of things you'd find at the bottom of lakes and rivers here on Earth.) What clues do these materials give you that water was once present? Get together with two classmates and brainstorm some ideas. Then, on a separate sheet of paper, write your "mission plan."

Solar System News

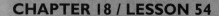

Moon Make-Up

Moons in our solar system are made of rock and ice. But how much of each moon is rock and how much is ice?

Many of the planets in our solar system have moons. Most moons are made of just rock and ice. Scientists determine what percentage of a moon is rock and what percentage is ice by using the moon's density. Density is the amount of matter in a given space. Imagine holding a rock in one hand and a piece of ice that is the same size in the other hand. The rock would feel heavier because rock is more dense than ice.

 **Activity**

DETERMINE ROCK-ICE PERCENTAGES

Use density to determine the percentages of rock and ice in the moons of the outer planets.

What You Need: pencil, calculator

What to Do:
The chart below shows how the percentage of rock in a moon determines the moon's density.
1. Use the data to make a line graph. The graph will show how a moon's density changes as the percentage of rock in it changes.

Percentage of Rock	Density of Moon (g/cm³)
100	average 3.5
80	3.0
60	2.5
40	1.9
20	1.4
0	0.9

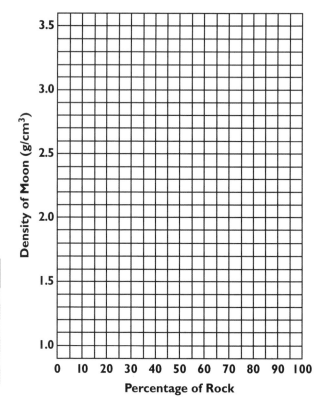

UNIT 5: ASTRONOMY

This chart lists the densities of the moons that orbit the outer planets in our solar system.

Planet	Moon	Density (g/cm³)	Percentage of Rock	Percentage of Ice
Jupiter	Io	3.5		
	Europa	3.0		
	Ganymede	1.9		
	Callisto	1.8		
Saturn	Mimas	1.2		
	Dione	1.4		
	Rhea	1.3		
	Titan	1.9		
Uranus	Miranda	1.4		
	Ariel	1.7		
	Umbriel	1.5		
Neptune	Triton	2.1		
Pluto	Charon	2.0		

2. For each moon in the chart, find the point on the graph that corresponds to the moon's density.
3. Use the graph to determine the percentage of rock the moon contains.
4. Calculate the percentage of ice the moon contains. (Hint: percentage of ice = 100% minus percentage of rock)

▶ Propose Explanations

ANALYZE DATA

▶ *What is the average density of rock?*

_____

▶ *What is the density of ice?*

_____

▶ *Explain why Mimas has both the lowest density and the highest percentage of ice.*

_____

_____

_____

_____

Picturing the Universe

A Star's Life

What can scientists tell about stars from their temperature and brightness? Plenty!

Birth. Infancy. Childhood. Youth. Middle age. Old age. These are some of the words used to describe the human life cycle. While stars are not living things, scientists describe them in terms of a life cycle, too. A star is born when a cloud of gas and dust comes together and begins to give off huge amounts of energy. As a star like our sun ages, it grows larger and cooler. At this stage it becomes a Red Giant. Later still, all that is left is a small white-hot core called a White Dwarf. At the end of its life cycle, a sunlike star cools even more to become a Black Dwarf.

 **Read**

NOTEZONE

Highlight any words or sentences you don't understand.

FIND OUT MORE

SCIENCESAURUS

SCILINKS
THE WORLD'S A CLICK AWAY

www.scilinks.org
Keyword: What is the
 life cycle of a star?
Code: GSED24

Curious about stars, Scott Basham of Orlando, Florida, wrote to an "Ask the Expert" Web site. An astronomer (a scientist who studies objects in space) named Terry D. Oswalt answered Scott's question.

Young and Old Stars

Scott Basham: How do we determine the life cycles of stars and tag some as "young" and some as "old"?

Terry Oswalt: This is one of the most important, and interesting, problems in astronomy.... It has taken astronomers most of...[the twentieth century] to piece together the life cycles of stars, simply because we cannot live long enough to follow a single star through its life cycle. Except in a few rare cases, most stars have looked the same as they do now since before humans began looking up at the sky.

Yet stars vary remarkably in their physical characteristics.... Do stars look different from one another because…they have different ages…? The key is to find a group of stars that has to be the same age.…

   Because it is highly unlikely that the stars in a cluster got together by accident, they must have been born at the same time.… When we compare…many different clusters, we find that those clusters which have many hot bright stars usually have some visible gas, suggesting that star formation may not be over. This type of cluster seldom has any Red Giants or White Dwarfs. In fact, the trend is that the fewer hot and bright stars a cluster has, the more Red Giants and White Dwarfs it has. The most likely cause of these differences is that different clusters have different ages—so we deduce that Red Giants and White Dwarfs are what stars become as they grow older.

tag: label
cluster: a group of stars that are close together in space
Red Giant: a large, very bright star that has cooled

White Dwarf: a small, very dense, hot, but faint star
deduce: conclude

From: "How Do We Determine The Life Cycles Of Stars And Tag Some As 'Young' And Some As 'Old?'." *Scientific American.*

199

INTERPRETING A MODIFIED H-R DIAGRAM In the early 1900s, two astronomers worked independently on the same problem. Enjar Hertzsprung worked in Denmark, and Henry Norris Russell worked in the United States. They both compared the brightness and temperature of stars. Brightness describes how much energy a star gives off. When they plotted brightness and temperature on a graph, a pattern appeared. (On the diagram below, brightness is given as a comparison with our own sun.) Today astronomers use a diagram based on their work. It is called the Hertzsprung-Russell diagram, or H-R diagram.

Notice that the temperatures on the horizontal axis go from highest on the left to lowest on the right. The numbers on the vertical axis compare the stars' brightness with the brightness of our own sun.

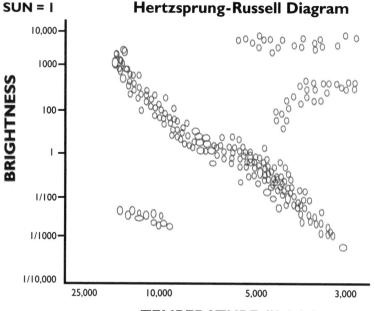

It seems logical that hotter stars would be more bright, and cooler stars would be less bright. Most stars, but not all, follow this pattern.

▶ *Find the large group of stars on the diagram that fit this pattern. Circle the group and label it "Main Sequence stars."*

Red Giant stars are very bright but very cool. They are bright because they are very large. Find the group of stars on the diagram that fits this description. Label them "Red Giant stars."

▶ *Do Red Giant stars fit the pattern shown in the Main Sequence? Why or why not?*

_____

_____

200

White Dwarf stars are very hot but very low in brightness.

▶ *Find the group of stars in the diagram that fit this description. Label them "White Dwarf stars."*

For most of their lives, stars have properties that put them on the Main Sequence part of the H-R diagram. A star stays in pretty much the same place within the Main Sequence for most of its life. At some point, its properties change and the star "moves" to a place above the Main Sequence on the diagram. Later, as it continues to change, it "moves" to a place below the Main Sequence.

▶ *Are Red Giants younger or older, compared with White Dwarfs?*

Astronomers have figured out that the hotter and brighter a star is to begin with, the less time it spends on the Main Sequence.

▶ *Which stars on the Main Sequence spend the least time as Main Sequence stars?*

ADD COLOR TO THE DIAGRAM If you live in a place away from city lights, you might notice that not all stars are the same color. Astronomers figure out the temperature of a star by analyzing the colors of light it gives off. Blue stars are hotter, and red stars are cooler.

▶ *Use a blue pencil or pen to color the stars on the H-R diagram with temperatures between 10,000 K and 25,000 K.*

▶ *Use green for stars with temperatures between 5,000 K and 10,000 K.*

▶ *Use yellow for stars between 3,000 K and 5,000 K.*

▶ *Use red for stars with temperatures lower than 3,000 K.*

▶ Propose Explanations

WHERE'S OUR SUN? When astronomers analyzed the color that our own sun gives off, they found it to be mostly yellowish green. Our sun's brightness places it on the Main Sequence. Its temperature is about 6,000 K.

▶ *Draw an arrow pointing to the area on the H-R diagram where our sun is located.*

▶ *What does our sun's position on the diagram tell you about where it is in its life cycle?*

Planet Search

What does it mean when a star's brightness dims? Something very interesting!

If planets form from the same gases and dust as stars do, then there are sure to be many, many planets in the universe. So the search for planets is on!

   Teamwork—that's what it takes to find planets beyond our solar system. More than a dozen teams of astronomers around the world are searching for planets. They point their telescopes at nearby stars and look for signs that a star might have planets orbiting it. The signs come slowly, sometimes over years. But the results are amazing. Earth may not be the only planet in the universe suited for life!

▲ **Artist's painting of a planet crossing in front of a distant star called HD 209458**

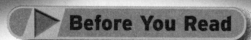

▶ Before You Read

SCIENCE TEAMWORK A few scientists work alone, but most scientists work in teams. Sometimes the people on the team work in the same building. Other times they work thousands of miles apart. Each member of the team has skills, knowledge, or tools that the others don't have. Together, the team members can solve problems that one scientist couldn't solve alone.

▶ *Describe a time when you were part of a team that solved a problem. What problem did you solve? How did each member of the team help solve it?*

_____

_____

_____

▶ **Read**

NOTEZONE

How did Henry know when to point his telescope at star HD 209458?

In 1999 astronomers saw a planet outside our solar system for the first time.

Team Sees Distant Planet

November 1999

A planet in another star system has been seen to cross the face of its parent star. The transit, as it is called, is the most direct glimpse yet of an extrasolar planet.

Over the past 4 years, several teams [of astronomers] have discovered more than two dozen extrasolar planets orbiting sunlike stars without actually seeing a single one. The astronomers inferred [the planets'] existence from slight [back and forth] movements of the parent stars, presumably [caused by] the tug of an orbiting planet.

On November 5, [astronomers Geoffrey] Marcy, Paul Butler, and Steve Vogt reported that they had detected a new set of telltale wobbles. As always, Marcy passed the new data on to [astronomer Greg] Henry, who uses small, automated telescopes...in Arizona to study sunlike stars [and look] for...planetary transits.

"When I saw Marcy's data for the star HD 209458," [Henry said], "I realized that a transit might occur in the night of November 7.... I quickly reprogrammed one of the automated telescopes before I went home." The next day, when Henry looked at the brightness measurements, he hardly believed what he saw. Exactly at the predicted moment, the star showed a brightness drop of 1.7%.

....

parent star: the star that a planet orbits
extrasolar: outside of our own solar system
wobble: a side-to-side movement

From: Schilling, Govert. "Astronomy: Shadow of an Exoplanet Detected." *Science.*

FIND OUT MORE

SCIENCESAURUS
Stars   245
Searching the Web 422

SCiLINKS
THE WORLD'S A CLICK AWAY

www.scilinks.org
Keyword: Telescopes
Code: GSED23

WHAT DO YOU THINK? Imagine taping a dime on a car's bumper next to the headlight. One dark night you see the car approaching from several blocks away. Its headlights are on.

▶ *Do you think you would be able to see the dime? Why or why not?*

_____

_____

_____

_____

▶ *How is this similar to astronomers looking for distant planets?*

_____

_____

_____

_____

LOOKING FOR WOBBLES With the tools they had in 1999, the California astronomers could not see the planet near star HD 209458. Instead, they looked for signs that a planet was affecting the star. Even a small planet's tug of gravity pulls on the star it orbits. As the planet orbits the star, it pulls on different sides of the star. This makes the star wobble.

After many mathematical calculations, the California team predicted when the planet might pass in front of star HD 209458. They called an astronomer in Tennessee and asked him to point a telescope in Arizona at the star.

▶ *What did the telescope in Arizona show?*

_____

▶ *Use the example of a dime and a car headlight as a model to explain what happened.*

_____

_____

_____

_____

THAT'S TEAMWORK!

▶ *What was the team of astronomers in California able to detect? How did they use that evidence?*

_____

_____

▶ *How was the astronomer in Tennessee able to help the team?*

_____

_____

_____

GENERATE QUESTIONS The planet described in the reading has a surface temperature of about 2,000°C (3,500°F). It is not likely to support life, but astronomers hope to find other planets that might. Think about the conditions that support life on Earth. List questions that scientists would need to answer in order to find out whether a far-off planet might support life.

_____

_____

_____

Take Action

DO ONLINE RESEARCH By the summer of 2002, astronomers had found evidence of more than 100 planets outside our solar system. Go online to find out how many planets scientists have now found beyond our solar system. Try searching by typing in these three keywords as one search: *extrasolar* (which means outside our solar system), *planet*, and *database*. What is the name and URL of a site you found? How many extrasolar planets are listed? Choose one of those planets and give its name. On a separate sheet of paper, list the information about it in the database.

Site name and URL _____

Number of extrasolar planets _____

Name of planet _____

Picturing the Universe

IMAGES FROM ENERGY

You can't see most kinds of energy from space, but you can use them to make images.

Your eyes can see only visible light. Visible light is part of the electromagnetic spectrum. The electromagnetic spectrum also includes other forms of energy that can travel through space, such as X rays, ultraviolet light, microwaves, and radio waves. All these other forms of energy are invisible to us.

Most telescopes can detect only part of the electromagnetic spectrum. Light telescopes, like the ones used to find distant planets, collect visible light. Using computers, astronomers create visible-light images that show how the object would look to the human eye if you could see that far away. Other telescopes detect the invisible forms of energy from space. For example, radio telescopes detect radio waves. These too can be made into images you can see.

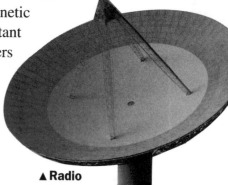

▲ Radio telescope

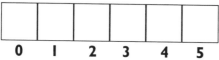
Activity

IMAGES FROM RADIO WAVES

Try making your own image from the energy detected by a radio telescope.

What You'll Need:
- radio telescope data sheet (Your teacher will provide this.)
- 6 colored pencils or markers, including black

What to Do:
1. Line up the colored pencils or markers and compare their brightness. (Hint: Squint your eyes or put the pencils or markers in the shade to help you see the brightness of the colors.) Move the colors around until you have arranged them from darkest to brightest.
2. To keep track of the order of the colors, fill in the key below. Use black for 0, the next darkest color for 1, and so on. The brightest color should be 5.

0	1	2	3	4	5

3. Use the key to color the boxes on the data sheet.

What Do You See?

▶ *What kind of space object does your image look like? (Hint: Look at pictures in an astronomy book or the astronomy chapter of a science textbook.) If you are still not sure what the object is called, describe how it looks.*

_____

_____

▶ *How is the image you made the same as your classmates' images? How is it different?*

_____

_____

▶ Propose Explanations

"TRANSLATE" YOUR IMAGE Each square you colored represents a point in space. The number in the square represents the strength of the radio waves detected by a group of radio telescopes.

▶ *What do you think 0 means? What do you think 5 means?*

FIND OUT MORE

SCIENCESAURUS

Stars, Galaxies, and
  Constellations 244
Galaxies   247

_____

The astronomers who make images from radio waves choose the colors they use for each image. The colors are not the colors you would see if you looked at the visible light from the space object.

▶ *Does it matter what colors you chose to create your radio telescope image? Why or why not?*

_____

_____

_____

▶ *What if you had used the brightest color for 0 and black for 5? Would you still have seen the shape of the object? Would you still know where on the image the most radio energy was? Explain.*

_____

_____

_____

Exploring Space

SAILING THROUGH SPACE

How can you sail without wind?

You may have seen pictures of rocket-powered spacecraft with fire and exhaust streaming out the back. As rocket fuel burns, gases push out of the rear of the spacecraft, and the craft is pushed forward. Scientists at NASA are searching for new ways to move spacecraft through space. One idea is to use a push from the sun instead of a push from rockets.

▲ Probe with solar sail

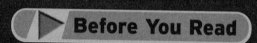
Before You Read

THE EFFECTS OF SUNLIGHT Think about the last time you went outside on a sunny day. How did sunlight affect objects on Earth? What changes did it produce? List some of the different ways that sunlight changes objects on Earth.

_____

_____

_____

_____

_____

_____

_____

_____

_____

_____

 **Read**

NOTEZONE

(Circle) an energy source that is used to push spacecraft through space.

Underline another way to push spacecraft that has not yet been tested.

NASA scientists are investigating ways to use sunlight to move spacecraft beyond our solar system.

Sailing to the Stars

Imagine being onboard a sailing ship. You unfurl the sails, set your navigation controls, and set sail for...the stars? That's exactly what we may be doing some day soon. Engineers and scientists are working on ways to build solar sails that will be pushed by sunlight. Just as sailboats on Earth don't need a motor and fuel, spacecraft with solar sails won't need rockets and rocket fuel.

All of the rockets we launch now use chemicals for fuel. When rocket fuel burns, it creates expanding gases that push out the end of the rocket engine. That pushes the rocket forward. But you have to carry a lot of rocket fuel with you if you want to travel to another star! Les Johnson, manager of Interstellar Propulsion Research at the Marshall Space Flight Center, says, "The difficulty is that rockets need so much fuel that they can't push their own weight into interstellar space. The best option appears to be space sails, which require no fuel."

So plans are to try a solar sail on a...[space probe]. The...sail will be nearly half a kilometer wide. The sail would be unfurled in space. Then, continuous pressure from sunlight would slowly speed up the probe until it's moving about five times faster than possible with regular rockets.

unfurl: spread open
navigation: steering
interstellar: among the stars
propulsion: being pushed forward

option: choice
probe: an instrument used to collect data

From: "Sailing to the Stars," *NASA Kids*. Center Operations Directorate at Marshall Space Flight Center. (kids.msfc.nasa.gov/news/2000/news%2Dsolarsail.asp)

Explore

HOW SOLAR SAILS WILL WORK Solar sail designs use solar energy, but not the way you might think. They don't change light into electricity like a solar cell does. They use the pressure of light. Light exerts pressure? Well, not a lot, but some. As particles of light, called photons, strike a surface, they put a tiny amount of pressure on it. If the light is reflected by the surface, the pressure on the surface is twice as great.

▶ *In order to get the greatest pressure, what sort of material do you think a solar sail should be made of?*

_____

_____

The force exerted by sunlight is very small. It doesn't push the solar sail very fast. But because sunlight will always be shining on the solar sail, the speed will slowly increase. Scientists predict that in time, the spacecraft will be traveling 90 kilometers per second (more than 200,000 mph)!

When objects such as airplanes and sailboats move through Earth's atmosphere, air resistance slows them down. Air resistance is caused by friction between the object and the air molecules it touches. But there is no air in outer space.

▶ *How can even a small push from sunlight be enough to move a space probe a great distance?*

_____

_____

_____

USING ANALOGIES The reading compares solar sails with the sails used on sailboats.

▶ *In what ways would a solar sail be like the sail on a sailboat?*

_____

_____

_____

▶ *In what ways would a solar sail not be like the sail on a sailboat?*

_____

_____

_____

© GREAT SOURCE. COPYING IS PROHIBITED.

ENERGY FOR SAIL

A rocket-powered spacecraft and a spacecraft with a solar sail use different energy sources.

▶ *How does using each energy source affect the weight of the spacecraft?*

_____

_____

_____

Objects outside our solar system are very far away. They are so far away that it would be much too expensive for a rocket-propelled spacecraft to carry enough fuel to reach them.

▶ *How might solar sails allow us to study distant stars and galaxies?*

_____

_____

_____

_____

_____

▶ **Take Action**

PLANETARY EXPLORATION Scientists know that other stars besides our sun have planets orbiting them. A probe with a solar sail might be able to reach one of those distant planets at some time in the future. What would you like to know about a probe's journey to another solar system? Write your questions below.

_____

_____

_____

_____

_____

_____

Exploring Space

IN FREEFALL

It's not exactly space travel, but it's close enough!

Being in space is not like being on Earth. Astronauts aboard a spacecraft orbiting far above Earth experience a feeling of weightlessness. This is because the spacecraft and everything inside it are in freefall—a constant falling motion in response to Earth's gravity. Before going into space, astronauts train to live and work in freefall. They do so by going into a freefall environment within Earth's atmosphere.

 **Read**

NOTEZONE

What questions do you have after reading this?

Former flight instructor Michael Long went to Russia to ride Ilyushin-76—an airplane used to create a freefall environment. On his airplane ride, Long experienced conditions like those felt by astronauts in space.

Preparing for Space

   The brilliantly white aircraft surges down the runway, engines screaming. [Once we reach the right] altitude, a steep 45-degree climb begins. Bright lights come on, and the pilot...lowers the nose of the airplane to produce about 30 seconds of [what feels like] weightlessness. Magically, we all rise like smoke and float and fly around. Just like that. People wriggling, eyes wide, mouths open, faces smiling, frowning. Bodies turning upside down—a stunning sight that my eyes record but that my brain seems unable to interpret. Major Boris V. Naidyonov of the Russian Air Force, my instructor, asks, "You OK?" He is concerned about nausea, and so am I. "I think so," I reply.
   ...One of my companions ricochets off the ceiling. Another does [floating] gymnastics. Naidyonov tosses me around the cargo bay like a javelin, twirls me like a baton. This is serious fun....

FIND OUT MORE

SCIENCESAURUS
Gravity   276

SCILINKS
THE WORLD'S A CLICK AWAY

www.scilinks.org
Keyword: Space Exploration and Space Stations
Code: GSED25

But [some of the other passengers] are silently vomiting into plastic bags.... They are experiencing the motion sickness that afflicts more than two-thirds of all astronauts upon reaching orbit....

surges: moves with a sudden burst of speed
interpret: understand the meaning of
nausea: the feeling of being sick to your stomach

ricochets: bounces
javelin: a long, thin bar designed for throwing through the air
baton: a short, thin bar designed for spinning
afflicts: affects

From: Long, Michael. "Surviving in Space." *National Geographic.*

 Explore

▶ *Why is it a good idea to put astronauts in a freefall environment before their real space flight?*

▶ *Imagine that the inside of a spaceship were like a room on Earth. What are some things that could be problems in a freefall environment?*

 **Take Action**

FREEFALLING Use the Internet or a library to research the inside of a spacecraft. Notice how it is built especially for a freefall environment. Draw the inside of the spacecraft below and label its special features.

Exploring Space

Why Explore Space?

Is space travel worth all the money we spend on it? You decide.

The United States government spends billions of dollars every year on space exploration. This money comes from taxpayers. Some people argue that we haven't gotten much for all that money. Others think that the journey itself is what's important, even if we don't find materials of value. Are the benefits of space travel worth the costs?

NOTEZONE

Underline Mr. Blevins's main points.

▶ **Read**

James Blevins of Wheatland, Wyoming, sent this letter to a science magazine.

In My Opinion

March 4, 2002

...The truth of the matter is that there is nothing out there [in space] that we know of that is of much value.... All of the planets are inhospitable enough that the only way a person could live on them would be in a bubble or space ship, so what is the point? We could get to Mars and maybe even find the remains of a microbe, so that we could know for sure there was life on other planets, but at what cost? If we are smart enough to get there, surely we must be smart enough to know that there is no reason to get there. There are so many problems here on Earth that the money could be used to solve.

inhospitable: unable to support life

microbe: an organism too small to see with the naked eye

From: Blevins, James R., Jr. "Concentrate on Earth." *The Scientist.* (www.the-scientist.com/yr2002/mar/let1_020304.html)

NOTEZONE

Underline the different "explorations" Mr. Collins lists in his letter.

John Collins of the Center for Environmental Research and Technology at the University of California sent this reply to Mr. Blevins's letter.

April 1, 2002

There's really no need to cut [dead] people apart to find out what's inside them either. After all, they're dead already. There's nothing you can do for them. And what are you trying to sail around the world for? You'll probably fall off the edge. Even if you do make it, you'll just wind up right where you started from. What a waste. Never mind that the computers used to send and receive your letter...are just one by-product of being stupid enough to send a man to the moon.

by-product: a result that was not intended

From: Collins, John F. "On Earth and Travel to Mars, I." *The Scientist.* (www.the-scientist.com/yr2002/apr/let_020401.html)

Explore

COMPARE AND CONTRAST

▶ *Summarize Mr. Blevins's argument in your own words.*

_____

_____

_____

_____

▶ *Summarize Mr. Collins's argument in your own words.*

_____

_____

_____

_____

TWO POINTS OF VIEW When people have strong ideas about an issue and are trying to convince others that these ideas are right, they often use reason or emotion to make their point. When using reason, they support their ideas with evidence. When using emotion, they try to stir up other people's feelings. Emotional arguments sometimes use sarcasm. In a sarcastic remark, a person says the opposite of what he or she means. Sarcasm is sometimes used to make fun of opposing ideas. Read the two letters again.

▶ *Which writer used reason in his argument?*

_____

▶ *Which writer used sarcasm?*

_____

▶ *How did he use sarcasm?*

_____

_____

_____

_____

▶ *Which person do you think made a stronger argument? (The stronger argument is not necessarily the one you agree with!) In what way was it stronger?*

_____

_____

_____

_____

_____

_____

_____

_____

_____

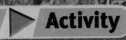

HOLD A DEBATE

Within every group of people, you will find differences of opinion. One way that people share different ideas is through a debate. A debate is not an argument. Each side is allowed to present its position without being disturbed. Then questions are asked and answered to explore the issue further. The most successful way to hold a debate is when both sides have logical, reasoned—not emotional—arguments. Hold a reasoned debate about whether space exploration is worth the cost.

What You Need: index cards

What to Do:

1. Form a team with classmates. Find out whether your team is assigned to be "for" or "against" space exploration.
2. With your teammates, brainstorm a list of points that support your assigned position. Write each point on an index card. For example, one point for space exploration might be "We might find valuable minerals on other planets." A point against might be "Space travel is risky, and sometimes astronauts die."
3. Put the cards in the order that best supports your team's position.
4. Hold a debate with the other side by taking turns presenting your points.
5. As the other team presents its side, write down any questions you want to ask them.
6. Ask the other team your side's questions. They will do the same to your team.

Write Reflections

▶ *What did you learn from the debate? Did the arguments you heard make you change your mind about anything? If so, what?*

_____

_____

_____

_____

_____

_____

_____

Glossary of Scientific Terms

A

air mass: a large body of air that has about the same temperature and humidity throughout it

air pressure: a measure of the weight of the atmosphere per unit of area on Earth's surface

altitude: height above average sea level

anemometer: an instrument that measures wind speed

asteroid: object made of rock, metal, and ice that is much smaller than a planet and that revolves around the sun; Most asteroids have orbits between Mars and Jupiter.

astronomy: study of space, including stars, planets, and other objects in space, and their origins

atmosphere: the layer of gases above a planet's surface

B

bacteria: one-celled organism that lacks a true nucleus

barometric pressure: *See air pressure*

C

carnivore: an animal that feeds on other animals, such as a wolf

cementation: process that turns sediments into hard rock when a binding material, often calcite, filters into the sediment

circumference: distance around a circle or sphere

climate: the general pattern of weather in a particular part of the world over a long period of time

cloud: group of tiny liquid water droplets hanging in the air

coal: solid fossil fuel, formed deep within Earth over millions of years

cold front: the leading edge of a mass of cold air; cold fronts can bring violent storms

comet: solar system object made mostly of ice, which follows a long, narrow orbit around the sun; A comet comes near the sun only occasionally.

compaction: process by which sediments are reduced in size or volume by pressure of rock or soil lying above them

condensation: the process in which matter changes from a gas to a liquid

conservation: the wise use and protection of natural resources

continent: any of Earth's seven large land masses

continental drift: theory that continents were once part of a single landmass that broke apart and moved to their present positions; led to the theory of plate tectonics

contour interval: difference in elevation between any two contour lines on a topographic map

contour line: on a map, line that connects points of equal elevation above sea level

coral reef: warm ocean ecosystem based on tiny animals called coral, which build a rock-like structure (reef) that shelters other organisms

crater: bowl-shaped hollow in the ground caused by a volcano or by a meteor strike

crust: outermost, rocky layer of Earth

crystal: solid made up of molecules arranged in a regular, repeating pattern

crystal structure: how the particles in a mineral or chemical are arranged

D

data: collected information, the results of an experiment or other investigation

density: a measure of mass per unit of volume; found by dividing the mass of the object by its volume

deposition: process by which wind, water, and gravity leave eroded sediments in new locations

dew point: the temperature at which water vapor changes to liquid

diameter: distance across a circle or sphere, measured through the center

dune: mound of sand that was deposited by wind

E

earthquake: energy waves passing through Earth, caused by a sudden shift along a fault line or by volcanic activity

echo: sound waves reflected off a surface

electrical energy: form of energy that consists of a flow of electric charges through a conductor

electricity: general term for interaction of electric charges

electromagnetic spectrum: full range of electromagnetic waves

elements: substances that are the building block of all matter; An element is made up of one kind of atom.

elevation: height above average (mean) sea level; also called **altitude**

energy: ability to do work

erosion: movement of weathered rock (sediment) by wind, water, ice, or gravity

estimate: an approximation or educated guess at a quantity, based on facts; also, the act of estimating

estuary: area where a river empties into the ocean and there is mixing of fresh water and salt water

evaporation: the process in which matter changes from a liquid to a gas

extinct: condition in which there are no more living members of a species

Glossary of Scientific Terms

F

fog: a cloud close to the ground

fossil: the remains, impression, tracks, or other evidence of an ancient organism

fossil fuels: fuels such as coal, oil, and natural gas; formed over millions of years from the remains of ancient plants and animals

G

galaxy: group of millions of stars; Earth is part of the Milky Way galaxy.

gas: matter that has no definite volume or shape, such as air

geology: study of Earth's structure, composition, forces, history, and future

geothermal energy: energy obtained from thermal energy inside Earth

glacier: large mass of ice and snow that exists year-round and is involved in erosion

global warming: an increase in the world's average temperature, possibly caused in part by fossil fuel use

grassland: large land region in which the main types of plants are grasses

gravity: force of attraction between any two objects

groundwater: water that collects and flows below the ground surface

H

hardness: relative ability of a solid, such as a mineral, to resist scratching

heat energy: total kinetic energy contained in all the particles of a substance

histogram: kind of bar graph used to show the frequency of values within a set of data

horizontal axis: a horizontal line marked with a scale that is used to place data points on a graph; sometimes called the x-axis

hurricane: a huge, slowly spinning tropical storm that forms over water and has winds of at least 119 km/h (74 mph)

hypothesis: an idea that can be tested by experiment or observation

I

igneous rock: rock formed from hot melted material that cooled

inference: an explanation that is based on available evidence but is not a direct observation

isobar: line on a weather map that connects points of equal air pressure

isotopes: atoms of the same element with different numbers of neutrons in the nucleus and thus different atomic masses; for example, carbon-12 and carbon-14

L

lava: molten rock material pushed up from a volcano or crack in the Earth; magma that has reached the surface

life cycle: all stages in the life of an organism or the existence of a star

liquid: matter that has a definite volume but not a definite shape; for example, water

M

magma: molten rock that makes up Earth's mantle and becomes igneous rock when it cools

mantle: a layer of Earth's surface, lying just below the crust and above the inner core

map: flat picture of part or all of the surface of Earth or another planet

map legend: list or explanation of symbols on a map

〰	**stream**
■	**house**
····	**unpaved road**
▦	**sandy area**

map scale: way of showing how distances on a map relate to distances on Earth's surface

matter: the material that all objects and substances are made of; anything that has mass and takes up space

metamorphic rock: rock that has been changed over time by high pressures and temperatures inside Earth's crust

meteor: a piece of rock from space that enters Earth's atmosphere and burns, creating a bright streak of light across the sky; **meteorite** is the part of a meteor that lands on Earth

meteorology: study of Earth's atmosphere

meteor shower: particles of rock and gas from a comet that burn up in Earth's atmosphere and can be seen as many streaks of light

microscopic: too small to be seen without a microscope

mid-ocean ridge: undersea mountain range that forms where two parts of Earth's crust are pushing apart (diverging plate boundary)

mineral: element or compound, formed by nature but not formed by living things, that has a specific crystal structure and physical and chemical properties

molecule: smallest particle of a substance that still has the properties of that substance

moon: a natural object that revolves around a planet

Glossary of Scientific Terms

N

natural gas: a fossil fuel; flammable, odorless gas (mostly methane) found in Earth

nonrenewable resources: natural resources that cannot be replaced once used, such as oil, coal, natural gas, and minerals

nutrient: substance that an organism needs in order to survive and grow

O

ocean current: flow of water within the ocean that moves in a regular pattern

oceanography: study of the physical properties of oceans and seas

orbit: path an object in space follows as it revolves around another object, such as Earth around the sun or a satellite around Earth

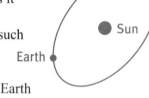

organism: a living thing

P

planet: a body in the solar system that is larger than several meters in diameter, does not produce large amounts of heat, and orbits only the sun

plate tectonics: theory that describes and explains the way that continents separated into today's land masses from one large ancestral land mass (Pangaea); also, the study of lithospheric plates, their movements, and Earth features that they affect

pollution: any change in the environment that is harmful to organisms

precipitation: water falling from clouds, such as rain or snow

prediction: a guess about what will happen under certain conditions, that is based on observation and research

pressure: amount of force exerted on a given area by an object or substance; SI unit is the pascal (Pa)

prevailing winds: winds that usually blow from only one direction

pyroclastic flow: ash, rocks, and similar solid material ejected from a volcano and rushing down its slope

R

radar: the use of reflected radio waves to determine the distance of an object and the direction it is moving

radioactive: giving off high-energy rays or particles

renewable resources: natural resources that can be renewed or replaced by nature, such as food crops and solar energy

reproduce: to make more individuals of the same species from a parent organism or organisms

rock: hard and compact mixture of minerals that formed naturally

rock cycle: process by which rocks, over geologic ages, are changed into different kinds of rock

runoff: water that flows over the ground surface

S

satellite: object that revolves around a larger object in space; The moon is a natural satellite of Earth; the Hubble Space Telescope is an artificial satellite.

sedimentary rock: rock formed when sediment is pressed and cemented together naturally over millions of years

sediments: tiny particles that settle out of water

soil: mixture of rock, mineral particles, and organic matter that forms at Earth's surface

solar energy: energy from the sun in the form of heat and light

solar system: the sun, its planets, and all other objects in orbit around the sun or planets

speed: distance traveled by an object in a given amount of time

star: huge object in space made up of gas and giving off light and heat from nuclear reactions; The sun is a star.

surface current: a river of water pushed along the ocean's surface by winds

T

technology: the use of scientific knowledge and processes to solve practical problems

temperature: measure of the average kinetic energy of the particles in a substance; measured in degrees Celsius (°C) or degrees Fahrenheit (°F)

theory: an idea that explains how many scientific observations are related

topographic map: map that shows the shape and elevation of the land surface using contour lines, and shows other land features using symbols and colors

topsoil: upper layer of soil, often the richest in plant nutrients

tornado: small, destructive, whirling, fast-moving storm that forms over land

transpiration: the process by which plants give off water vapor through their leaves

V

vertical axis: a vertical line marked with a scale that is used to place data points on a graph; sometimes called the y-axis

volcano: hill or mountain formed by material that erupts onto Earth's surface; caused by action of magma below surface

volume: amount of space an object or substance takes up; measured in liters (L) or cubic centimeters (cm³)

W

water cycle: cycle in which water moves through the environment, through the processes of evaporation, condensation, and precipitation

watershed: area of land that catches precipitation and channels it into a large body of water, such as a lake, river, or marsh.

wave: a back-and-forth motion that travels from one place to another

wavelength: distance from any point on one wave to a corresponding point on the next wave, such as crest to crest or compression to compression

weather: conditions in the atmosphere, including humidity, cloud cover, temperature, wind, and precipitation

weathering: process by which water, wind, and ice wear down rocks and other exposed surfaces; includes chemical and mechanical weathering

wind: movement of the air caused by differences in air pressure